DATE DUE

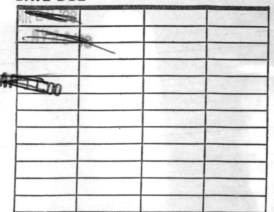

Modern Critical Interpretations

John Millington Synge's
The Playboy of the Western World

Modern Critical Interpretations

These and other titles in preparation

Modern Critical Interpretations

John Millington Synge's

The Playboy of the Western World

Edited and with an introduction by

Harold Bloom
Sterling Professor of the Humanities
Yale University

Chelsea House Publishers ◊ *1988*

NEW YORK ◊ NEW HAVEN ◊ PHILADELPHIA

Printed and bound in the United States of America

10 9 8 7 6 5 4 3 2 1

∞ The paper used in this publication meets the minimum
requirements of the American National Standard for
Permanence of Paper for Printed Library Materials,
Z39.48–1984

Library of Congress Cataloging-in-Publication Data
John Millington Synge's The playboy of the western world /
    edited and with an introduction by Harold Bloom.
        p. cm.—(Modern critical interpretations)
    Bibliography: p.
    Includes index.
    Contents: The making of the playboy / Patricia Meyer
Spacks—The dramatic imagination / Alan Price—A hard
birth / Donna Gerstenberger—Character and symbol /
Robin Skelton—Approaches to The playboy / Nicholas
Grene—The playboy as antidrama / Bruce M. Bigley—The
"gallous" story and the dirty deed / Edward Hirsch—The
living world for text / Hugh Kenner.
    ISBN 1-55546-031-3 (alk. paper): $19.95
    1. Synge, J. M. (John Millington), 1871–1909. Playboy of
the western world. [1. Synge, J. M. (John Millington),
1871–1909. Playboy of the western world. 2. English
literature—History and criticism.] I. Bloom, Harold.
II. Series.
PR5532.P53J64 1988
812'.912—dc19   87–27461
                                                      CIP
                                                       AC

Contents

Editor's Note

This book brings together a representative selection of the best critical interpretations of John Millington Synge's comic drama *The Playboy of the Western World*. The critical essays are reprinted here in the chronological order of their original publication. I am grateful to Johann Pillai and Henry Finder for their assistance in editing this volume.

My introduction centers upon Christy Mahon's self-transformation in reaction to his own language. Patricia Meyer Spacks begins the chronological sequence of criticism by observing wisely that *The Playboy* "seems a work destined to be forever misinterpreted," partly because it is both realistic and fantastic.

Benign wit mingled with palpable irony and dramatic contrast are seen by Alan Price as the imaginative constituents of Synge's masterwork, while Donna Gerstenberger centers upon the genesis and development of the play. Robin Skelton sets forth the Christy/Christ analogue, after which Nicholas Grene emphasizes that *The Playboy*'s meanings are complex and uncertain.

Antidrama is Bruce M. Bigley's genre for the play, in sharp contrast to Edward Hirsch, who finds two intensely dramatic visions in conflict—fantastic farce and critically realistic social commentary. The distinguished Modernist critic Hugh Kenner concludes this volume with a formalist appreciation of Synge's attempt to write a prose as intricate and dramatic as any verse.

Introduction

Eighty years after its riot-provoking first performance (1907), Synge's *Playboy of the Western World* retains an extraordinary freshness. Whether or not it was or is an accurate representation of peasant life in the impoverished rural west of Ireland seems rather unimportant. What matters is the play's aesthetic originality and power as a kind of phantasmagoric farce, vitalistic in its ideology, anticlerical in its parodistic drive, and exalting the persuasiveness of rhetoric over the reductive world of the reality principle.

Synge's *Playboy,* as a stage comedy, has important debts to Shakespeare, Ben Jonson, and Molière, and a closer relationship to the exuberant vitalism of that savage visionary, Yeats, but its originality is the most salient quality that a rereading establishes. A reader is likelier to think of Sean O'Casey, Synge's successor, than of Synge's own precursors. In *Playboy,* Synge triumphantly made it new, partly by an art of perspectivism learned from Molière and partly by an almost Chaucerian and Shakespearean genius for representing the change of a character who changes precisely by listening to his own language. Christy Mahon is transformed by overhearing himself, and his extraordinary metamorphosis in act 3 is one of the glories of modern drama.

Allegorizations of Synge's *Playboy* generally fail, not because they venture too much, but because they tend to be timid and mechanical. Christy Mahon does not seem to me a parody either of Christ or of Oedipus, though his parodistic relationship to Cuchulain, hero of Ireland and of Yeats, is clear enough. But so original is Synge's mode of visionary farce that parody becomes phantasmagoric reality, and the spirit of Cuchulain inhabits Christy throughout act 3. Cervantes hovers near, and Synge himself invoked Don Quixote as relevant to Christy Mahon. Celtic chivalry, brutal in its

1

rhetoric and in its myths, returns from the repressed in *The Playboy of the Western World,* a drama never likely to be popular with Irish Catholic audiences, whether in Eire or America.

One paradox of the Irish dramatic tradition is that it is Protestant; another is that it celebrates not only Protestant individuality but Romantic vitalism, even when it at last reaches the abyss, in *Waiting for Godot, Endgame,* and *Krapp's Last Tape.* From the title until its extraordinary final lament, the *Playboy* is one of the most extravagant ironies ever to be played upon the stage. The "Western World" turns out to be northwest Mayo, hardly in 1907 a breeding ground for playboys. When, at drama's end, Pegeen Mike pulls her shawl over her head, we hear a somewhat surprising lamentation: "Oh my grief, I've lost him surely. I've lost the only Playboy of the Western World." The surprise is that the charming young Pegeen, only a few moments before, has blown up the fire with a bellows, so as to lift up a lighted sod in order to scorch the Playboy's leg, while he is pinned down on the floor by her companions. One doubts that the Dublin and American riots against the *Playboy* really were caused by Christy's celebrated image of "a drift of chosen females, standing in their shifts itself, maybe, from this place to the Eastern World." Synge's image of west Ireland is joyous in its presentation, but what it reflects is barbaric squalor, credulity, brutal cupidity—a world of drunken louts and their hopelessly desperate women.

The only exception is Christy Mahon himself, one of the most curious heroes that even modern drama has engendered. For two acts he is scarcely an improvement over those he has come among, and at first we do not like him any better when he enters, dressed as a jockey, after his offstage triumphs in act 3. His courtship of Pegeen is then conducted in the rhetoric of a lowlife Tamburlaine, and he is as piteous as ever when his perpetually resurrected father, the old Mahon, rushes in upon him. Synge's finest moment is the epiphany of Christy's transformation after Pegeen turns against him, for reasons just as bad as first moved her towards him:

> CHRISTY (*to Mahon, very sharply*): Leave me go!
> CROWD: That's it. Now Christy. If them two set fighting, it will lick the world.
> MAHON (*making a grab at Christy*): Come here to me.
> CHRISTY (*more threateningly*): Leave me go, I'm saying.

MAHON: I will maybe, when your legs is limping, and
your back is blue.

CROWD: Keep it up, the two of you. I'll back the old
one. Now the playboy.

CHRISTY (*in low and intense voice*): Shut your yelling, for
if you're after making a mighty man of me this day
by the power of a lie, you're setting me now to
think if it's a poor thing to be lonesome, it's worse
maybe to go mixing with the fools of earth.
(*Mahon makes a movement towards him.*)

CHRISTY (*almost shouting*): Keep off . . . lest I do show a
blow unto the lot of you would set the guardian angels winking in the clouds above.
(*He swings round with a sudden rapid movement and
picks up a loy.*)

CROWD (*half frightened, half amused*): He's going mad!
Mind yourselves! Run from the idiot!

CHRISTY: If I am an idiot, I'm after hearing my voice this
day saying words would raise the topknot on a poet
in a merchant's town. I've won your racing, and
your lepping, and . . .

MAHON: Shut your gullet and come on with me.

CHRISTY: I'm going, but I'll stretch you first.
(*He runs at old Mahon with the loy, chases him out of
the door, followed by crowd and Widow Quin. There is
a great noise outside, then a yell, and dead silence for a
moment. Christy comes in, half dazed, and goes to fire.*)

WIDOW QUIN (*coming in, hurriedly, and going to him*):
They're turning again you. Come on, or you'll be
hanged, indeed.

CHRISTY: I'm thinking, from this out, Pegeen'll be giving
me praises the same as in the hours gone by.

That low and intense voice in which Christy celebrates the power of a lie marks the incarnation of a new self in him, a self that might
even be called (as it was in the eighteenth century) the Poetical Character. When Christy comes in, half dazed, it is with the repeated,
mistaken belief that *this time* he indeed has murdered his father. He
proceeds to continue his absurdly Romantic quest for Pegeen until he

suffers the horror of her fall from imagination:

> CHRISTY: What ails you?
>
> SHAWN (*triumphantly, as they pull the rope tight on his arms*): Come on to the peelers, till they stretch you now.
>
> CHRISTY: Me!
>
> MICHAEL: If we took pity on· you, the Lord God would, maybe, bring us ruin from the law to-day, so you'd best come easy, for hanging is an easy and a speedy end.
>
> CHRISTY: I'll not stir. (*To Pegeen.*) And what is it you'll say to me, and I after doing it this time in the face of all?
>
> PEGEEN: I'll say, a strange man is a marvel, with his mighty talk; but what's a squabble in your back-yard, and the blow of a loy, have taught me that there's a great gap between a gallous story and a dirty deed. (*To Men.*) Take him on from this, or the lot of us will be likely put on trial for his deed to-day.
>
> CHRISTY (*with horror in his voice*): And it's yourself will send me off, to have a horny-fingered hangman hitching his bloody slip-knots at the butt of my ear.
>
> MEN (*pulling rope*): Come on, will you?
>
> (*He is pulled down on the floor.*)
>
> CHRISTY (*twisting his legs round the table*): Cut the rope, Pegeen, and I'll quit the lot of you, and live from this out, like the madmen of Keel, eating muck and green weeds, on the faces of the cliffs.

From playboy to mad outcast is the rhetorical gesture, but the psychic reality is that the nastily pragmatic Pegeen has just stimulated Christy into falling out of love, which Iris Murdoch splendidly reminds us is one of the great human experiences, causing us to see the world again with awakened eyes. After battling bravely and almost gaily against the whole pack of Mayo men and suffering Pegeen's judicious efforts with the hot sod, Christy greets Old Mahon with a marvelous humor: "Are you coming to be killed a third time, or what ails you now?" Soon enough, resurrected father and newly born son are reconciled, with their former authority relationship reversed, and Christy bestows a final blessing upon the louts and dionysiac women he leaves behind him:

> CHRISTY: Ten thousand blessings upon all that's here, for
> you've turned me a likely gaffer in the end of all,
> the way I'll go romancing through a romping life-
> time from this hour to the dawning of the judg-
> ment day.
> (*He goes out.*)
> MICHAEL: By the will of God, we'll have peace now for
> our drinks. Will you draw the porter, Pegeen?
> SHAWN (*going up to her*): It's a miracle Father Reilly can
> wed us in the end of all, and we'll have none to
> trouble us when his vicious bite is healed.
> PEGEEN (*hitting him a box on the ear*): Quit my sight.
> (*Putting her shawl over her head and breaking out into
> wild lamentations.*) Oh my grief, I've lost him surely.
> I've lost the only Playboy of the Western World.

He goes out, and the spirit of romance goes with him, leaving the unhappy Pegeen with her cowardly betrothed and with the Western World of Father Reilly. To call Synge sardonic is weak and inadequate, if only because the apotheosis of Christy from timid brat to roaring boy has a Marlovian persuasiveness about it. Synge took the large dramatic risk of linking the imagination to familial violence in a purely comic context. *The Playboy of the Western World,* his masterwork, places Synge securely between Wilde and Shaw, just before him, and O'Casey and Beckett, coming after. To have written a comedy as original as *The Importance of Being Earnest* or *Pygmalion,* and as dark in its nihilistic implications as *Juno and the Paycock* or *Endgame,* is an astonishingly integrated achievement.

The Making of the Playboy

Patricia Meyer Spacks

Yeats said of *The Playboy of the Western World* that the inability of the original audiences to understand it represented the only serious failure of the Abbey Theatre movement. The most recent significant appearance of *The Playboy* took place off-Broadway in 1958, and its reviewers, though generally kind, revealed, like those of the past, some confusion as to the essential import of the play. Indeed, *The Playboy* seems a work destined to be forever misinterpreted. At the start of its career in 1907 it caused riots because of its alleged immorality; since then it has produced mainly perplexity. Seeing a realistic production of *The Playboy,* one is made acutely conscious of the problem which Synge himself raised during the first tumultuous week of the original Dublin performance, when he insisted he'd written "an extravaganza"—only to add later that the source of the play lay in his understanding of Irish psyche and Irish speech as they actually existed, thus claiming for the work an ultimate realism.

The dilemma of whether *The Playboy* is essentially realistic or fantastic is the one on which producers and critics have foundered ever since. Viewed as realistic drama, the play immediately begins to seem implausible. That a man should become to strangers a hero by virtue of a tale of patricide, and become in the end genuinely masterful for no readily apparent reason—the psychology of the real world is little help in interpreting these events. On the other hand, if one considers the play as fantasy, it begins to seem strangely random and undeniably hampered by its realistic elements. *The Playboy*

From *Modern Drama* 4, no. 3 (December 1961). © 1961 by the University of Toronto, Graduate Centre for the Study of Drama.

has usually been admired for its quaintness, its poetry, or its comic force, and, though a popular anthology piece and reasonably often revived, has been universally underrated as a coherent work of art. I do not plan a full reading of it here, but wish to trace a source of the play's power which has never been insisted upon by critics or producers.

One aspect of *The Playboy* that seems disturbing is the curious tone with which it treats the theme of patricide. To be sure, the second time Christy strikes his father the spectators on stage feel that he should be hanged for his deed. But they are in no way horrified by it: they believe Christy to be potentially dangerous to them and they fear legal involvement in his crime; self-preservation motivates them. Nor, for that matter, does the revived father appear to think that there is anything extraordinary about a son who has twice tried to kill him. He resents the attempts in a personal way—as well he might—but he does not find them unnatural. The emotional weight of *The Playboy of the Western World* is on patricide as a noble deed, not as an abhorrent one.

Oedipus kills his father, and the crime brings a plague on his city. Orestes kills his mother and is pursued by furies. Patricide and matricide were for sophisticated Greeks the most dreadful of sins; Freud has brought modern readers to consciousness of the roots of the horror which the Greeks felt, and which twentieth-century audiences of Greek tragedy continue to feel. Yet Synge somehow manages to treat so dreadful a theme with apparent lightness. For parallels to this sort of treatment, one must go to the folk tale. The pages of Grimm are full of violence: giants who eat their victims, blood and bones; enchanters who turn the unwary to stone; kings who demand the impossible and cut off the heads of those who fail to achieve it. Irish folk tales, of course, deal with the same sort of material; their heroes wade through blood to prove themselves. To be sure, this violence has a somewhat factitious quality: one is always aware that those who are turned to stone will become flesh and blood again at the end; that the frog, once its head is cut off, will turn into a prince; that however many anonymous warriors are slaughtered along the way, the true hero will accomplish the impossible and not be slaughtered himself.

In *The Playboy*, too, extreme violence is in a sense unreal. Both "murders" take place off stage. Moreover, neither of them really takes place at all: twice the father, in effect, rises from the dead, as people rise from the dead in fairy tales. Yet the symbolic violence, as in a fairy tale, shapes and defines the story: without his attempts to murder his father, one cannot imagine Christy becoming a man. One finds the same sort of pattern in many folk tales. In "The Battle of the Birds," an Irish fairy tale for which parallels exist "throughout the Indo-European world," the king's son has to undergo a series of tests before he can win Auburn Mary as a bride. Last of all, he must obtain five eggs from the top of a 500-foot tree. To get the eggs, Mary tells him, he must kill her, strip the flesh from her bones, take the bones apart, and use them as steps for climbing the tree. The prince is reluctant, but the girl insists; after the task is completed, she is rejuvenated from scattered bones and becomes his wife. The murder of the girl, then, is totally unreal, yet it is absolutely essential for the hero's winning of her.

The necessity for violence in the process of testing and maturing is, of course, frequently emphasized in folk tales: it is for precisely this reason that some modern censors have doubted the suitability of such tales for children's reading. The hero must cut off, on three successive days, the three heads of the "Laidly Beast"; or he must fight first a giant with one head, then a giant with two heads, then a giant with three heads. We feel that such obstacles are important mainly as tests, hindrances of increasing complexity and difficulty which must be overcome on the road to maturity. Ritual bloodshed is both necessary and significant: blood must be shed before the child becomes a man, before the nonentity becomes a hero. And the strange attitude toward father-murder in *The Playboy* is explainable in exactly the same way. The frivolity with which the first murder is treated is justifiable on the ground that it never in actuality takes place: it is more obviously unreal than a fantasy of murdered giants. But more importantly, the attitude of the playwright toward the murder is justifiable because the murder itself is justifiable—and more than justifiable: even necessary. It is a ritual murder, a step in the process toward maturity.

Certainly there is no question that Christy grows before our very eyes in *The Playboy*. The frightened boy who comes on stage in the first act, looking nervously about him, asking if the police are likely to come, miserably gnawing a turnip before the fire, is quite different from the Christy who departs in the last act. He leaves the stage with these words: "Ten thousand blessings upon all that's here, for you've turned me a likely gaffer in the end of all, the way I'll go romancing through a romping lifetime from this hour to the dawning of the judgment day." He recognizes the change in himself, and blesses the tavern company for having brought it about. But the responsibility is his, not theirs, and the transformation has been accomplished through the successive murders of his father.

Characteristically in the folk tale, actions, tests, come in groups of three. The prince in "The Battle of the Birds" undergoes three tests; Conn-Eda, whose story is retold by Yeats, has to procure three magic objects; the young gardener in "The Greek Princess and the Young Gardener" has to obtain not only the golden bird he first set out for, but also the king of Morocco's bay filly and the daughter of the king of Greece. In this play, too, there are three tests, three ritual murders, not merely two, and the development of Christy's character takes place through them. The Christy with whom the play begins is described by his father, in the boy's absence, as "a dirty, stuttering lout." Christy is, old Mahon continues, "a liar on walls, a talker of folly, a man you'd see stretched the half of the day in the brown ferns with his belly to the sun." He is lazy, frightened of girls, "a poor fellow would get drunk on the smell of a pint," with a "queer rotten stomach." He is the laughingstock of all women; the girls stop their weeding when he comes down the road and call him "the looney of Mahon's."

There is something familiar about this characterization: we have here the foolish son of so many fairy tales, the male equivalent of Cinderella. Sons, in folk tales, also usually appear in threes. Two of them are reputed to be clever and brave, but they fail when they undertake the crucial quest. The youngest son is scorned by all, thought unworthy even to attempt the quest, considered foolish and stupid and cowardly, the one least likely to succeed. "A poor woman had three sons. The eldest and second eldest were cunning clever fellows, but they called the youngest Jack the Fool, because they thought he was no better than a simpleton." Given a fairy story that starts this way, one can easily predict its ending: Jack the Fool will ultimately triumph, achieving what his elders have been unable to accomplish. And the same prediction can be made about Christy.

We are told that he has brothers and sisters, and that they have not been able to free themselves from their father, even after escaping from home and leaving Christy alone with old Mahon. "He'd sons and daughters walking all great states and territories of the world," Christy says, "and not a one of them, to this day, but would say their seven curses on him, and they rousing up to let a cough or sneeze, maybe, in the deadness of the night." They are not truly free, not free as Christy in the end is free: in the nights they wake to curse their father. It remains for Christy, the foolish son, to subdue the father once and for all.

The first "murder" is nearly an accident, and its maturing effects are stumbled upon by accident. Christy strikes his father almost in self-defense, after an argument over whether he is to marry the rich old widow his father wants for him. He tells his story in the tavern largely because his pride is touched by the suggestion that he is wanted by the police for commonplace reasons. His true realization of what the murder means grows only gradually, fostered by the reactions of those to whom he tells his story. Soon, as a result of it, he comes to think of himself as, in effect, a poet: the equation between poetry and violence remains constant throughout the play. "I've heard all times it's the poets are your like," Pegeen says, "fine fiery fellows with great rages when their temper's roused." The image appeals to Christy, and becomes his picture of himself. To himself, to the rest of the world, he had hitherto seemed, in his own words, "a quiet, simple poor fellow with no man giving me heed." But now, to himself and to the rest of the world, he is a "fine fiery fellow"—a poet and a hero. Christy has apparently achieved freedom and power with the greatest ease: he remarks himself that he was a fool not to have killed his father long before. His new assurance carries him to triumph in the games even though his father has actually appeared before then: he relies on the Widow Quin to protect him, and assumes that people's belief in him as a father-murderer is as good as the reality.

But when Christy and his father are brought into conjunction, in the third act, it becomes immediately clear that manhood is not so easily won. The old man starts beating his son, and the passive Christy is reviled and ridiculed by all. His grandiose self-image is destroyed: he defends himself finally not on the basis of his achievement, but because he has never hurt anyone, except for his single blow. But the man of no violence, as Christy is soon brought to see, is no poet and no hero; he is the eternal victim, the scapegoat. Understanding for the first time what failure means, he can no longer accept it willingly. His rejection by the company makes Christy see that his earlier success has been an illusion, based, as he says, on "the power of a lie," and that he has substituted for loneliness the company of fools. Yet the effects of the first "murder" make the second one possible: Christy bolsters himself with the memory of his physical and rhetorical triumphs and, so strengthened, dashes out to kill his father again.

W. H. Auden has suggested that one of the distinguishing characteristics of the fairy tale is its stress on the power of the wish: the wish is the main cause of fairy tale events. "The cause of all wishes is the same," he writes—"that which is should not be. . . . When a scolded child says to a parent, 'I wish you were dead,' he does not mean what he actually says; he only means 'I wish I were not what I am, a child being scolded by you.' " Christy's attempts to murder his father are fairy-tale-like enactments of such a wish: not so much that the old man should be dead as that he, Christy, should no longer be in a position to be humiliated by his father—and, by extension, humiliated by the rest of the world. But the second "murder" is different from the first. The first is a spontaneous reaction to humiliation; the second is a calculated and aware reaction. The wish has turned to will: Christy has perceived—or thinks he has perceived—that actual violence is necessary for social acceptance. And violence, after all, is still a simple matter. He has but to strike his father once again, and the impossible will be accomplished: Pegeen will be properly won, and Christy will be at last truly free.

The blow is struck, and Christy expects his reward, as the fairy-tale hero after each trial is likely to think that trial the last. The Widow Quin warns him that he will be hanged, but he indignantly rejects the suggestion. "I'm thinking," he says, "from this out, Pegeen'll be giving me praises the same as in the hours gone by." And, a bit later: "I'm thinking of my luck to-day, for she will wed me surely, and I a proven hero in the end of all." But it is Pegeen herself who drops the rope over his head, Pegeen who calls his act "a dirty deed," Pegeen who burns his leg as he lies bound on the floor. For Pegeen and the others this "killing" has none of the symbolic richness of the "gallous story" Christy told of his first murder, the story which seemed to identify him as a man of great stature and great passions. The storyteller as hero is another familiar figure in Irish folk lore. In "Conal Yellowclaw," the hero wins freedom for his three doomed sons by telling three stories; "The Story-Teller at Fault" constructs an elaborate fiction around the dilemma of a storyteller with no tale to tell. And Christy as man in action seems less heroic than Christy as storyteller. The second attack on his father has been too transparently motivated by the desire for approval; it is in no way heroic. Christy's mistake, however, is rectified as a result of the attack on him it causes. The first "murder" made the second one possible, in typical fairy-tale fashion, and so does the second bring about the third. For as a result of being totally rejected by those who have previously praised him, Christy discovers for the first time that he doesn't *need* these fools.

The third "murder" takes place before our eyes, and is entirely verbal and symbolic in its enactment: Christy discovers he can give his father orders, shove him out the door, tell him that their relation now is to be that of "a gallant captain with his heathen slave." Having achieved, as a result of experience, genuine self-confidence, he can manage a real triumph, without violence, and one not based on a lie or motivated by desire for approval. Christy has yearned to escape the domination of his father and others; he fulfills his wish at last in appropriate terms, freeing himself not by physical murder, but by asserting his own power to dominate. The stupid son has become a hero, has inherited the kingdom and claimed his rights as ruler. If, contrary to the convention of the fairy tale, he does not win the princess, it is only because she is not worthy of him: he could have her now that he scorns her. It is Pegeen, indeed, who underscores his triumph, breaking into lamentations for her loss of one who, she realizes at last, is after all "the only Playboy of the Western World."

The word "playboy" is defined, in effect, by the action of the drama; it comes finally to mean the hero in the sense of a man who can "play" successfully with language, triumph in the "play" of athletic contests, excel in the "play" of flirtation and courtship. As he leaves the stage for the last time, Christy has become a playboy indeed, the man and the pose finally identical. And here the word "playboy" is used of him for the first time without ironic overtones. It has previously been employed to stress the disparity between Christy's pose and the actuality. The word is first spoken by Widow Quin, laughing at Christy, who has been huddled in terror behind the door while she talks with his father. She observes, "Well, you're the walking Playboy of the Western World, and that's the poor man you had divided to his breeches belt." The Widow Quin uses the word a second time in the context of Christy's victory in the games, still with the irony of her superior awareness. She tells old Mahon that the people are cheering "the champion Playboy of the Western

World," and the old man is thereby led to think that this could not possibly be his worthless son. The fact that Christy's father is still alive is revealed to the crowd, and they jeer at the lad by calling out, "There's the playboy!" And when, in the curtain speech, Pegeen wails, "Oh my grief, I've lost him surely. I've lost the only Playboy of the Western World," the import of the phrase depends upon our knowledge of its previous ironic uses. Now at last it is spoken without irony, and now at last it *can* be applied without irony: Christy has won the right to the title.

Pegeen's final lamentations are preceded by her final rejection—with a box on the ear—of Shawn, her official suitor. Shawn, the true fool of the play, points up by contrast all the way through not only the superior richness of Christy's character, but the importance to that character of the father-murders. Father-destruction is, after all, an archetypal theme, and the primitive *necessity* of father-murder is stressed in *The Playboy* by the character of Shawn, who is totally unable to free himself from authority. He pleads for himself, in the second act, that he doesn't *have* a father to kill. But Shawn is clearly—and ridiculously—dominated by a father-figure, the priest, Father Reilly. When other characters in the play refer to Shawn, it is almost always in conjunction with Father Reilly; the lad is notoriously under the thumb of the priest, whose authority he is always citing, and of whom he is admittedly afraid. The priest is his excuse for lack of courage and imagination, for unwillingness to do the unexpected. None of his neighbors respect him; his subjection is too complete. Pegeen's father admits that he'd rather have Christy's children for grandsons than Shawn's, who would be only "puny weeds." The man who is dominated is a weakling; he must assert his individuality—must metaphorically kill his father—before he is to be respected. Both positively and negatively, then, the point is stressed. The idea of father-murder is the thematic center of the play, a center with precisely the sort of mythic overtones that are so often found in folk tales.

The ritual power of the "murders" in the play is reinforced by the ritual power of the language. Susanne Langer has suggested the essential similarity between the symbolism of metaphor and the symbolism of ritual; a sense of this intimate relation between language and ritual dominates *The Playboy of the Western World*. If it can be said that Christy is created as a man by his successive "murders" of his father, it can be said with equal truth that he is created by the force of language. The murder of his father represents, from the beginning, a sort of metaphor of achievement; Christy's verbal metaphors also define a pattern of achievement. Symbols are brought to life in this play in a rather special way. It has been commonplace, at least since Freud, that for primitive people the relation between word and thing is close, that the magic of spells depends upon the notion of this close tie. In *The Playboy* language seems to have power in the real world, as spells have power—as language in the folk tale has power. As Christy develops self-command, he develops also command of language; his increasingly poetic speech reflects his increasingly imaginative perception, and with the final subduing of his father comes a final control of language. Yet in another sense it might be said not that Christy comes to control language, but that language comes to control him.

The idea of himself as a poet, suggested by Pegeen, comes to have great importance for Christy; it is for him and the others inextricably connected with the idea of the hero. When the young man makes his first appearance, his speech has the strong folk rhythm of all the characters and some flashes of imagination, but he is essentially prosaic. Deciding to stay, he says, "It's a nice room, and if it's not humbugging me you are, I'm thinking that I'll surely stay." His reaction, in short, is that of the practical man—or the man trying to be practical. Left alone with Pegeen, after the suggestion that he is a poet has been made, he describes his father "going out into the yard as naked as an ash tree in the moon of May, and shying clods against the visage of the stars till he'd put the fear of death into the banbhs and the screeching sows." The father flings clods at the stars and gets a response from pigs; the disproportion between stimulus and response here suggested marks the situation of Christy himself, a dreamer by inclination whose life has hitherto been bounded by the most mundane details. Stars and moon are the typical material of his expanding metaphors. Pegeen, annoyed with him, seems to drive him away; as he goes to the door, he describes himself as "lonesome, I'm thinking, as the moon of dawn," and Pegeen is won to call him back. His metaphors grow more extravagant as his confidence develops. He speaks of Pegeen as having "the star of knowledge shining from her brow," and connects her repeatedly, in his references to her, with "the heavens above." In the wooing scene, he appeals to her with elaborate images of love-making beneath the moon and stars, and insists on the superiority of Pegeen to anything offered by the Christian heaven: he talks of "squeezing kisses on your puckered lips, till I'd feel a kind of pity for the Lord God in all ages sitting lonesome in his golden chair." Finally, at the height of Christy's first illusory triumph, Pegeen's father reports Father Reilly as saying that the dispensation has come in the nick of time, so he'll wed Pegeen and Shawn in a hurry, "dreading that young gaffer who'd capsize the stars." There has been no evidence that Father Reilly is an imaginative man; indeed, he seems to stand for all that is opposed to imagination. When he makes this comment about Christy, we feel as though the youth's most extreme metaphors have become fact, have formed the facts: as though it were indeed conceivable that Christy should overturn the stars, unlike his father, whose attempts at the stars only arouse the farm animals. Similarly, in a slightly earlier scene, old Mahon, not recognizing his son, comments, "Look at the mule he has, kicking the stars." Christy has somehow been created a true giant—and created partly by the power of his metaphors.

The same pattern of development from prose to extravagant poetry is repeated in miniature in the brief scene between Christy's humiliation by his father and his second murder attempt. It is repeated again, with a difference, between the second "murder" and the third. Once more, Christy's language develops in power as the lad develops in self-realization, but this time the self-realization is successful, and the language has an entirely new quality. No longer dependent on the opinion of others, Christy gains a new freedom; his speech, too, gains new freedom, a quality of pure joy different from anything it has had before. He talks of hell now as he had talked of heaven, but without the sense of unreality that clings to his earlier metaphors. The fusion of joy and reality that Synge spoke of as one of his goals in the play is complete at the very end. Christy leaves us with his vision of "a romping lifetime," couched in romping language.

So *The Playboy of the Western World* presents essentially the vision of a man constructing himself before our eyes. Not only does Christy construct himself: he creates his princess. Pegeen is, after all, a matter-of-fact girl with a hot temper. But she is not that sort of girl after a conversation with Christy. As Christy's images grow more and more compelling, Pegeen becomes more and more gentle and eloquent herself. She, too, seems to be changing before our eyes. Finally she comments on the phenomenon: "And to think it's me is talking sweetly, Christy Mahon, and I the fright of seven townlands for my biting tongue. Well, the heart's a wonder." But it seems to be the sheer power of language that has won Pegeen, and she apparently recognizes the fact herself when she says she'd not wed Shawn, "and he a middling kind of a scarecrow, with no savagery or fine words at all."

The importance of the idea of Christy as a constructed man is stressed by the fact that it is the main source of the play's humor as well as of its serious import. The comedy of *The Playboy* depends heavily on the ironic conjunctions between the felt ritual importance of the Playboy's role and the evidence of his incompetence or pettiness in the real world. The girls come to do him homage, bearing gifts, deducing from his boots that he is one who has traveled the world; they find him indulging in petty vanity with the looking glass. Christy describes himself as "a gallant orphan cleft his father with one blow to the breeches belt"; immediately afterwards he staggers back in terror at the sight of his living father. The young man is enjoying his triumph; his father comes in and starts beating him. Over and over the device is employed, to insist on Christy's efforts to make appearance and reality coincide, the name of hero correspond to the actuality. And as the central action of the ritual "murders" is reflected by the patterns of Christy's language, so the ironic conjunctions of the action are symbolized by such verbal patterns as the one we have noted around the word "playboy."

The sense of the fairy tale which one is likely to get from *The Playboy* does after all, then, provide clues for a reading of the play which solves the problem of the relation between realism and fantasy in it, and also suggests the sources of its strange power. The themes, the language, the import of the play resemble those of folk tale and myth; its "serious" aspects and its comic ones alike, it seems, may be largely accounted for by this relation.

The Dramatic Imagination:
The Playboy

Alan Price

In *The Well of the Saints* we see the tension between dream and actuality with the imagination, the major force working on this tension, used by Martin to escape from it. In *The Playboy of the Western World* we see the same tension with the imagination the major force working on it, but in this case Christy's imagination transforms the dream into actuality. If Keats's cry: "lord, a man should have the fine point of his soul taken off to become fit for this world," may be thought of as an apt gloss on *The Well of the Saints,* another saying of his: "The Imagination may be compared to Adam's dream—he awoke and found it truth" is well exemplified in the main theme of *The Playboy.*

The actuality in the opening of *The Playboy* is the terrified weakling, Christy. An impetus to imaginative activity on his part is given by the admiration of the villagers when they hear his tale. They present to his imagination a dream or ideal picture of himself, and his imagination becomes creative. It works upon himself, that is upon the original actuality, and as the play goes on the raw material of the Christy of the opening scene is shaped by the power of the imagination in accordance with the dream or ideal presented by the villagers, until by the end of the play Christy actually is the daring playboy that the villagers thought him to be at first. The actuality of the first scene is transformed by the dream into a new actuality, and in the end the dream and the actuality are one. Christy wakes and finds his dream

From *Synge and Anglo-Irish Drama.* © 1961 by Alan Price. Russell & Russell, 1972.

truth. This is in direct contrast to the end of *The Well of the Saints* where the dream and actuality are at complete variance.

Synge starts by creating the kind of situation in which such a transformation would be most likely to take place; he presents a soil and climate most apt to welcome vigour and imagination, and to make them blossom. With the exception of Shawn and, presumably, Father Reilly, everyone living in the small, remote Mayo village is stifled by the drabness of existence and longs for action and excitement. The people are not altogether lacking in capabilities: Pegeen is pretty and spirited; there is a capacity for enjoyment in Michael James; Philly is cunning and shrewd; and Jimmy has a tender sensibility. Yet they can find no outlet for their energies, except in drinking bouts. Even these are beyond the feeble Shawn, whom Pegeen is going to marry. He is the only young man available—all the vigorous young men seem to have emigrated—and he merely moves Pegeen to tease or scold him.

Upon this inert community certain disorderly groups impinge; Pegeen declares: "Isn't there the harvest boys with their tongues red for drink, and the ten tinkers is camped in the east glen, and the thousand militia—bad cess to them—walking idle through the land." The villagers fear the savagery of these people, and yet, somehow, are attracted by it; so that, when they hear that a queer strange fellow is roaming nearby, all conclude that he is dangerous. Shawn is asked to stay to protect Pegeen, but he refuses, not so much because he is afraid of being hurt but because he is scared of a rebuke from Father Reilly if he spends any time alone with a young woman at night:

> Let me out. . . . Oh, Father Reilly, and the Saints of God, where will I hide myself today. . . . Leave me go, Michael James, leave me go, you old Pagan . . . or I'll get the curse of the priests on you, and the scarlet-coated bishops of the Court of Rome.

After the spectacle of a lover too fearful of upsetting his priest to look after his fiancée, Pegeen and Michael James are ripe to applaud any sign of enterprise, however unusual, and the appearance of a daring young fellow who has prevailed against the authority of his father is welcome. Thus, Synge skilfully and amusingly prepares the entrance of Christy and sets him down where he is most likely to be appreciated—among people who, finding life intolerably dull, are avid for sensation.

Christy provides the sensation. Yet, entering, he seems quite incapable of doing so. But this is part of Synge's method of establishing Christy, at first, as a downtrodden, inoffensive creature, in order that his eventual transformation may be the more marked and glorious. Accordingly Christy creeps in, so tired and frightened and dirty that any people less starved of incident than the villagers would have ignored him. To them, however, he is of interest, particularly when he betrays anxiety about the police. The villagers question him, but, although he begins to feel a little flattered by being, for the first time in his life, an object of attention, he reveals nothing. His evasive answers increase their curiosity and pleasure; they sense a mystery; and when, partly to retain their attention, partly under Pegeen's skilful examination—which plays upon his pride by denying his achievement—he abruptly confesses, no one is disappointed. Their admiration is heartfelt: "There's a daring fellow." His first account of the deed is unadorned: "I just riz the loy and let fall the edge of it on the ridge of his skull, and he went down at my feet like an empty sack, and never let a grunt or groan from him at all." The matter-of-fact tone of this, and the gentleness of Christy's demeanour—he protests that he is "a law-fearing man" and not "a slaughter-boy"—impress the villagers more then a deal of boasting would have done. They are awed by the feeling that there are mysterious forces in this slight figure, and they think that this lad who speaks so humbly and reasonably of slaying his dad, and sits peacefully with his drink, "should be a great terror when his temper's roused." Moreover, their dislike of the police and the belief that the police would be scared of Christy are additional recommendations; and Christy soon has their approval so firmly that they readily put a favourable construction on all he says and does. Also, as Jimmy points out, the villagers need a brave man:

> Bravery's a treasure in a lonesome place, and a lad would kill his father, I'm thinking, would face a foxy divil with a pitchpike on the flags of hell. . . . Now, by the grace of God, herself will be safe this night, with a man killed his father holding danger from the door, and let you come on, Michael James, or they'll have the best stuff drunk at the wake.

The men go out, Pegeen contemptuously dismisses Shawn, and then begins to take possession of Christy and to beam on him; and the seed, in a favourable environment for the first time, begins to bud under her warmth.

Pegeen holds before him an image of "a fine handsome fellow with a noble brow," who has the qualities of the great poets of the past, "fine fiery fellows." Christy's significant rejoinder (contrasting well with the rounded cadences of most speeches) conveys his delight and surprise perfectly: "Is it me?" It is not he yet, but it will be. Christy finds some difficulty at first in recognizing himself in Pegeen's image, but every instinct urges him not to cast doubts upon it, but to believe in it and confirm it. "Expanding with delight at the first confidential talk he has ever had with a woman" he begins to see the day on which he struck his one blow as a crucial moment in his life. Before, he had been merely existing, disdained by all, and unaware of his own powers: "Up to the day I killed my father, there wasn't a person in Ireland knew the kind I was, and I there drinking, waking, eating, sleeping, a quiet, simple fellow with no man giving me heed." In common with most of those characters in Synge who are imaginative, and like persons with a particular kind of poetic temperament, Christy found solace only in the natural world:

> I after toiling, moiling, digging, dodging from the dawn to dusk; with never a sight of joy or sport saving only when I'd be abroad in the dark night poaching rabbits on the hills . . . and there I'd be as happy as the sunshine of St Martin's Day, watching the light passing the north or the patches of fog, till I'd hear a rabbit starting to screech and I'd go running in the furze. Then, when I'd my full share, I'd come walking down where you'd see the ducks and geese stretched sleeping on the highway.

But he was continually beset by one horror—his father:

> He after drinking for weeks, rising up in the red dawn, or before it maybe, and going out into the yard as naked as an ash tree in the moon of May, and shying clods against the visage of the stars till he'd put the fear of death into the banbhs and the screeching sows . . . he a man never gave peace to any, saving when he'd get two months or three, or be locked in the asylums for battering peelers or assaulting men.

Christy's vivid picture of Mahon serves at least four purposes: it establishes Mahon as a giant whom Christy has killed, thus giving Christy a source of endless self-congratulation, and providing evidence on which his imagination can feed; it helps to make Christy's eventual transformation even more credible, since Mahon is so savage there is at least the possibility that his son will have some savagery in him; it depicts Mahon as a villain, one whom the villagers would consider deserved death, particularly in view of his lasciviousness; it helps to prepare for the eventual entrance of Mahon. The memory of the monster whom he has overcome excites Christy further: the "tap of the loy" of some minutes previously is now a skull-splitting blow, and Christy regards himself as "a fine lad deserves his good share of the earth . . . a seemly fellow with great strength and bravery." Widow Quin's hammering on the door at this instant produces terror in Christy, but his collapse is only temporary. When he sees two fine women quarrelling over him his admiration for himself reaches new heights, and the dream moves another step towards actuality. Furthermore, this clash, marked by Pegeen's eloquent invective and Widow Quin's craft, makes it clear that Christy has come to the spot where there is scope and appreciation for quickness of fancy, fine talk and daring; and well might he say as he nestles in bed: "it's great luck and company I've won me in the end of time—two fine women fighting for the likes of me—till I'm thinking this night wasn't I a foolish fellow not to kill my father in the years gone by."

This mood is sustained and strengthened at the opening of act 2. For the first time in his life Christy is enjoying himself and beginning to perceive and prize qualities in himself which he had not been conscious of before:

> Well, this'd be a fine place to be my whole life talking out with swearing Christians, in place of my old dog and cat; and I stalking around, smoking my pipe and drinking my fill, and never a day's work but drawing a cork an odd time, or wiping a glass, or rinsing out a shiny tumbler for a decent man. . . . Didn't I know rightly, I was handsome . . . and I'll be getting fine from this day, the way I'll have a soft lovely skin on me and won't be the like of the clumsy young fellows do be ploughing all times in the earth and dung.

The subsequent passage in which some village girls worship Christy as a hero has been objected to as mere padding, but it seems to me to have a function. It gets the act under way in a fresh and engaging manner, yet without startling—tension should, and does, come later; it shows how widespread is the ennui and how strong the craving for excitement in the village—Christy has become a sensation overnight—it motivates Pegeen's annoyance with Christy later in the act; and it provides good comedy. The passage also mirrors the behaviour of some people towards persons of notoriety. These girls who peep through a crack at Christy, who touch his bed with awe and try his boots on, who acclaim him with all the superlatives at their command, and who beseech him to take their offerings, have counterparts among us today. Popular journalism has given them an appetite for the lurid, and they (not unlike the crowd at a murder trial) are "after rising early and destroying themselves running fast up the hill" to gaze on a man who has done a deed of violence.

A little later Widow Quin enters, and, after making herself very agreeable to Christy, pleases him further by asking him to relate how he did his deed. This he does, with great relish, demonstrating his actions by means of a half-eaten leg of chicken in one hand and a mug of tea in the other. When he reveals that the quarrel started on his refusal to follow his father's wishes by marrying a venomous hag, their sympathy and admiration for him are complete. Spurred on by this most amiable audience he presents the action (which now to his mind, as to theirs, is of heroic proportions) with dramatic and bloody detail: "I hit him a blow on the ridge of his skull, laid him stretched out, and he split to the knob of his gullet. (*He raises the chicken bone to his Adam's apple.*)" The girls are in ecstasies at this, but Pegeen's entry ends the performance. The girls are sent packing, Widow Quin, after a brisk encounter with Pegeen, retreats, and Christy is left alone to face Pegeen's anger. The next passage is, by contrast to what has gone before, sombre, and displays a depth of feeling untouched in the play previously.

Among the impulses behind Christy's mainly instinctive desire to make himself like the image that has been presented to him, the conscious drive has been the wish to impress Pegeen. She played a major part in exciting his imagination with this image, and he wishes to prove to her (as well as to himself) that he really is the same as the image. In this shaping process he is getting into touch with actuality, and becoming aware of certain powers in his nature which were lying dormant until the force of the imagination brought them into activity. Now, faced by Pegeen's anger, Christy experiences a kind of fear and distress unknown to him before; if she withdraws her protection and inspiration he feels that he will never make the image actual, and that he will undergo pain and disappointment unexperienced previously. His character is developing rapidly, and accordingly the opportunities for happiness and sorrow, the rewards and punishments are becoming greater. He is in the middle way; he can never go back to his former undeveloped condition, and his new personality is only in the process of being formed. He still needs the right audience and the stimulus of Pegeen's admiration. In the days before his deed he welcomed solitariness; but now he dreads it; and he sets forth his fears in a precise image from Irish life:

> It's a lonesome thing to be passing small towns with the lights shining sideways when the night is down, or going in strange places with a dog noising before you and a dog noising behind, or drawn to the cities where you'd hear a voice kissing and talking deep love in every shadow of the ditch, and you passing on with an empty, hungry stomach failing from your heart.

Pegeen can hardly accept this; like all the villagers she treats any admission of weakness in Christy as a mere subterfuge to cloak some daring design; she is puzzled; but she can see that he is genuinely in love with her, and that he is convinced of the dangers of confiding in other women, so she becomes kinder and more attentive than ever. She is declaring that she "wouldn't give a thraneen for a lad hadn't a mighty spirit in him and a gamey heart" when Shawn rushes in.

The contrast between Shawn and Christy is marked most effectively, when, having got rid of Pegeen by a trick, Shawn and Widow Quin try to persuade Christy to leave. In his own community in Meath Christy was probably as weak and despised a creature as Shawn is here, but now Christy, made masterful by imagination, rejects Shawn's offer with scorn, and swaggers out to try on the fine new clothes. Christy's first essay in arrogance, fortunately against weak opposition, is overwhelmingly successful. Shawn's desperation produces one of the most amusing speeches in the play:

> Oh, Widow Quin, what'll I be doing now? I'd inform against him, but he'd burst from Kilmainham and he'd be sure and certain to destroy me. If I wasn't so God-fearing,

> I'd near have the courage to come behind him and run a
> pike into his side. Oh, it's a hard case to be an orphan and
> not to have your father that you're used to, and you'd easy
> kill and make yourself a hero in the sight of all.

Amusing, too, is the fact that Shawn's best clothes help to make
Christy more handsome and imposing, thus impressing the villagers
further, and increasing still more Christy's self-esteem. The fall from
this height of pride is set forth with considerable skill. Christy's
rotund rhythms boasting of a blow of epic grandeur, his grandiose
struts and frets and gestures, change instantly to sharp phrases of
horror and a terrified scramble into a hiding-place, as Old Mahon
appears:

> CHRISTY: From this out I'll have no want of company
>   when all sorts is bringing me their food and cloth-
>   ing, the way they'd set their eyes upon a gallant or-
>   phan cleft his father with one blow to the breeches
>   belt. (*He opens door, then staggers back.*) Saints of
>   Glory! Holy Angels from the throne of Light!
> WIDOW QUIN: What ails you?
> CHRISTY: It's the walking spirit of my murdered da!
> WIDOW QUIN: Is it that tramper?
> CHRISTY (*wildly*): Where'll I hide my poor body from
>   that ghost of hell?

Christy is now more desperate than was the despised Shawn a few
moments earlier; and the comic effect of the contrast is driven home
by Old Mahon's descriptions of his son as "a dirty stuttering lout . . .
and ugly young blackguard."

Synge's skill is seen in contriving that Widow Quin should be
the one to meet Old Mahon and to learn the truth. Any other character would have published the truth at once; Pegeen, for instance,
would have sent Christy off lonely on the roads or back to subjection,
and the transformation from dream to actuality would have been
incomplete. But the wily Widow Quin sees that she may turn this
knowledge to her own advantage, and she tries to persuade Christy
to give up Pegeen and to marry her. This is the great moment of
temptation and decision for Christy; acceptance of Widow Quin's
proposals would be the safe course but would involve the surrender
of his imagination, since he would have to cut himself off from the
main conscious source of his inspiration—Pegeen—and he would no

longer be able to believe in himself as a daring young hero; the image would be shattered, and the transformation from weakling to champion playboy would not take place. It is not suggested that Christy deliberated in his mind about these matters—he was probably not fully aware of them, and his choice was an intuitive one—but the whole tone and tenor of the play gives us cause to entertain the notion that this passage is, among other things, emblematic of the temptation, which must often come to the emergent artist, to leave his work half-finished, and to turn away to what appears to be ease and safety.

Christy, however, is true to his dream, and he rejects Widow Quin's suggestions, persuading her instead to help him keep Old Mahon out of the way:

> WIDOW QUIN: If I aid you will you swear to give me a
>   right of way I want, and a mountainy ram, and a
>   load of dung at Michaelmas, the time that you'll be
>   master here?
> CHRISTY: I will, by the elements and stars of night.
> WIDOW QUIN: Then we'll not say a word of the old fel-
>   low, the way Pegeen won't know your story till the
>   end of time.

Thus, Christy is lifted from this trough through the power of his imagination and the cooperation of Widow Quin; and by the end of the act, as he leaps out to the sports, he is rehabilitated and more eager than ever to prove to all that he is a wonder.

When we see Christy again he is at the height of his public fame and fortune, though still protesting that all his triumphant deeds at the sports are insignificant compared to his killing of his dad. So great is his feeling of power and exultation that he has quite forgotten that his dad is still alive and near at hand. The love-scene which follows shows that the transformation is approaching completion. The man who makes love with such ardour is a different person from the shy recluse of Meath, different from the abject, then flattered, fugitive of act 1, and different even from the boaster of act 2. He actually possesses those qualities which Pegeen and the others fancied they saw in him at first, and there is a confident energy in his rhythms and an assured exactness in his imagery that have not been marked in his speech before. The passage has most of the features usually found in Synge's dramatic poetry, and here they are wrought to a peak of splendour and dramatic effectiveness.

An indication of Synge's quality may be gained from noting some lines from Douglas Hyde's *Love Songs of Connacht* which Synge probably had in mind. Hyde says: "I had rather be beside her on a couch, ever kissing her, than be sitting in heaven in the chair of the Trinity." Synge gives us: "I squeezing kisses on your puckered lips, till I'd feel a kind of pity for the Lord God is all ages sitting lonesome in His golden chair." Synge's choice of words is more accurate and evocative: passionate kisses are "squeezed" and the lips must be "puckered"; and there is, as Oliver Elton says, "a melodious and passionate extravagance"—which aptly conveys Christy's extreme joy—in Synge's transformation of the notion of lovers preferring their joys to those of heaven. At the opening of the passage both Christy and Pegeen are happy but shy, as if expecting a crucial declaration of their feelings. When this is made each inspires the other to further eloquent expressions of devotion, and towards the climax the speeches (all of about the same length and with a similar rhythmic flow and cadence) give the impression of ritual, one lover praising the other in perfect measure and time. There is nothing mawkish about this duet, and consequently it is enhanced rather than damaged by the immediate contrast with another kind of richness and reality, by being ended with the entrance of Michael James "swamped and drownded with the weight of drink." Shawn helps him in but the mere sight of Shawn is sickening to Pegeen, and Christy chases him off. The climax of the happiness of Christy and Pegeen comes now, as Michael James gives them his blessing, in a speech which summarizes the qualities the villagers admire Christy for:

> It's the will of God, I'm thinking, that all should win an easy or a cruel end, and it's the will of God that all should rear up lengthy families for the nurture of the earth. What's a single man, I ask you, eating a bit in one house, and drinking a sup in another, and he with no place of his own, like an old braying jackass strayed upon the rocks? (*To Christy*) It's many would be in dread to bring your like into their house for to end them, maybe, with a sudden end; but I'm a decent man of Ireland, and I liefer face the grave untimely and I seeing a score of grandsons growing up little gallant swearers by the name of God, than go peopling my bedside with puny weeds the like of what you'd breed, I'm thinking, out of Shaneen Keogh. (*He joins their*

hands.) A daring fellow is the jewel of the world, and a man did split his father's middle with a single clout should have the bravery of ten, so may God and Mary and St Patrick bless you, and increase you from this mortal day.

The fall from this height is the most severe that Christy undergoes. The entrance of Old Mahon casts him in a few seconds from the peak of delight down to a depth of anguish and despair which makes all his former troubles mere trifles. And this time there is no one to help him. Previously when his confidence had been shaken Pegeen or Widow Quin had helped to stimulate and nourish his imagination and thus to restore his faith in himself. But now Widow Quin can do nothing, and Pegeen, very hurt and disappointed, begins to assail him, while Michael James and the crowd, feeling that they too have been cheated, join in. For some moments Christy is desperate:

> And I must go back into my torment is it, or run off like a vagabond straying through the unions with the dust of August making mudstains in the gullet of my throat; or the winds of March blowing on me till I'd take an oath I felt them making whistles of my ribs within?

But he is developing every minute; the stress, the pressure, now harden not dissolve him; and the jeers of the crowd instead of breaking him (as they would have done at any time previously) make his transformation almost complete. There is a brief moment of imaginative activity, then the truth comes to him, and, as a man who has proved himself superior to all around, he speaks with authority to the crowd, now in a frenzy at the prospect of a fight: "Shut your yelling, for if you're after making a mighty man of me this day by the power of a lie, you're setting me now to think if it's a poor thing to be lonesome it's worse, maybe, go mixing with the fools of the earth." He then charges through the mob and rushes out to strike down Old Mahon.

Christy's first words on returning reveal the conscious motive behind this act, as behind all others in the play so far: "I'm thinking, from this out, Pegeen'll be giving me praises, the same as in the hours gone by." He is not a weakling or a charlatan, he knows now; he has beaten every man in the sports, overthrown Shawn, wooed and won Pegeen in a way that any fiery poet of the old world could hardly surpass, and he has felled his dad. He actually is all that the villagers thought him to be, a hero; and he expects Pegeen to recognize this.

But it is now Christy who is in love with a dream, and it is Pegeen who falls far short of Christy's image of her. For she herself is mainly responsible for the capture of Christy; she alone hitches the rope over his head, thereby giving Shawn his solitary moment of joy in the play—"Come on to the peelers, till they stretch you now."

"Me," roars Christy, "I'll not stir." He then directs his last appeal to Pegeen: "And what is it you'll say to me, and I after doing it this time in the face of all?" But she rejects him unreservedly:

> I'll say, a strange man is a marvel, with his mighty talk; but what's a squabble in your back yard, and the blow of a loy, have taught me that there's a great gap between a gallous story and a dirty deed. (*To men*) Take him on from this, or the lot of us will be likely put on trial for his deed today.

This is the bitterest blow Christy has to face, the last test and the severest, and for a moment the anguish of this disillusionment, along with the vivid imaginative apprehension of death, almost shatter his newly created personality:

> And it's yourself will send me off, to have a horny-fingered hangman hitching slip-knots at the butt of my ear. . . . Cut the rope, Pegeen, and I'll quit the lot of you, and live from this out, like the madman of Keel, eating muck and green weeds on the faces of the cliffs.

It seems that having come so far Christy is to fail at this last extremity; dream and actuality will disintegrate just as they were about to become one. Then (by a masterly piece of dramatic irony) Pegeen, this time against her will, saves Christy, and makes the transformation complete. Previously her admiration and affection had inspired Christy; now her coldness, her unjust taunts, move him to resolute and effective action. She calls him "a saucy liar," and cooperates with Shawn to torture and capture him. At this Christy's spirit bends to his full height, and he becomes completely transformed:

> PEGEEN (*blowing the fire with a bellows*): Leave go now,
>   young fellow, or I'll scorch your shins.
> CHRISTY: You're blowing for to torture me. (*His voice
>   rising and growing stronger*) That's your kind is
>   it? Then let the lot of you be wary, for, if I've to
>   face the gallows, I'll have a gay march down, I tell
>   you, and shed the blood of some of you before I
>   die.

Thus, at the supreme crisis, Pegeen has abandoned Christy and has joined the others against him. Their feelings for each other, which found such consummate expression in their duet only a few minutes earlier, die as Pegeen blows the fire to burn Christy, and as he, realizing the truth about himself and her, hisses out: "That's your kind is it?" words, in their simple directness, contrasting effectively with the rich fervour of the love duet.

The making actual of the image, fullness of stature, self-realization, independence, all come together. Now Christy fears nothing; his spirits mount as he feels his strength; he actually is the Playboy, the wonder of the west, a Samson compared with the villagers who vainly try to hold him down, and against whom he roars rich and colourful defiance:

> CHRISTY: If I can wring a neck among you, I'll have a
> royal judgement looking on the trembling jury in
> the courts of law. And won't there be crying out in
> Mayo the day I'm stretched upon the rope, with la-
> dies in their silks and satins snivelling in their lacy
> kerchiefs, and they rhyming songs and ballads on
> the terror of my fate? (*He squirms round on the floor
> and bites Shawn's leg.*)
> SHAWN: My leg's bit on me. He's the like of a mad dog,
> I'm thinking, the way that I will surely die.
> CHRISTY: You will, then, the way you can shake out
> hell's flags of welcome for my coming in two
> weeks or three, for I'm thinking Satan hasn't many
> have killed their da in Kerry, and in Mayo too.

Pegeen's final act against Christy (not done without some pity) does not touch his heart, but causes him much pain, so that he kicks and flings around until he comes face to face with Old Mahon. This is a wonderful climax. Father and son, both on hands and knees, stare at each other for a moment while the truth sinks in: that Christy is now master—as his first words show: "Are you coming to be killed a third time, or what ails you now?" The older order has gone for ever; the son is emancipated, and in the new relationship he is the dominant figure:

> CHRISTY: Go with you, is it? I will then, like a gallant
> captain with his heathen slave. Go on now and I'll
> see you from this day stewing my oatmeal and

> washing my spuds, for I'm master of all fights from
> now. *(Pushing Mahon)* Go on, I'm saying.

Old Mahon's reply to this is a further example of Synge's excellence:
"Is it me?" he says, thereby echoing exactly Christy's words in act 1.
At that early stage Pegeen presented to Christy the image of the
daring poet she thought him to be, and which he was to become.
Christy's "Is it me?" then marked the beginning of his recognition of
a new situation and the beginning of his transformation. Now at the
end of the play image and actuality are one, and the "Is it me?" of act
1 is now "It *is* me." Likewise Old Mahon's "Is it me?" marks the
beginning of a new situation, he realizes that from this out he is to be
the subordinate partner. And his feelings about this are similar to
those of Christy in act 1: surprise not unmingled with delight. For his
son has made good, he is not an idle weed, he is a true Mahon; and
Old Mahon, having had his reign, is pleased to resign his authority
into such worthy hands; Old Mahon, too, is at last happy. Christy's
delight in his power and distinction and his confidence in a splendid
future, do not prevent him from giving due thanks and praise: in
success he remains likable. He alone knows that Pegeen and the villagers have, unwittingly, helped to "make a mighty man of him by
the power of a lie," and his last words are of gratitude: "Ten thousand blessings upon all that's here, for you've turned me into a likely
gaffer in the end of all, the way I'll go romancing through a romping
lifetime from this hour to the dawning of the Judgement Day."
     Pegeen's grief is (naturally) that she has lost Christy, the only
Playboy, and it might be said that she lost him because, at the crucial
moment, her belief in the image collapsed; ironically enough, just at
the moment when it was palpable that the image had become actual.
In those moments when Christy realized that the image was truth,
Pegeen shut her eyes to it. If Christy's development through the play
may be thought of as an illustration of Keats's observation: "The
imagination may be compared to Adam's dream—he awoke and
found it truth," Pegeen's behaviour may be thought of as emblematic
of the attitude of the person who denies the validity of imaginative
experience as a moral agent and as an avenue to truth. She rejects
Christy and calls him "a crazy liar" because he has been responsible
for her belief in a fiction: that Christy killed his father. She fails to see
that by means of this fiction acting upon Christy's imagination her
image of a daring poet has become truth. Christy at the end really is

the daring poet she believed him to be, and he has become that without killing his father. But Pegeen refuses to see the new actuality. She regards only the old fiction; she is blind to the *end* and fails to see that the fiction was the *means* to this end; a fiction, moreover, in which no one consciously deceived anyone else, which brought only good, no harm. The play, then, embodies ideas of some consequence, as Synge explains; "it is not a play with 'a purpose' in the modern sense of the word, but although parts of it are, or are meant to be, extravagant comedy, still a great deal that is in it, and a great deal more that is behind it, is perfectly serious when looked at in a certain light."

In important respects *The Playboy of the Western World* and *The Well of the Saints* are complementary—there is sameness with difference—and both plays together present a fairly comprehensive treatment of the workings of the imagination. Both embody several degrees of blindness to, or awareness of, dream and actuality; instances of deception occur, but the conscious deception brings unhappiness when confronted with actuality (in *The Well of the Saints*), while the unconscious deception, the poetic fiction, helps to create a new and better actuality and to bring happiness (in *The Playboy*). It has been said that there is a good deal of the artist in Martin Doul; the same can be said of Christy. All that we learn of Christy, both before and after the blow, indicates that he has the powers of the artist and an outstanding ability to use words. Even Old Mahon has to admit that Christy has facility of tongue and fancy: "a murderous gob on him . . . he a lier on walls, a talker of folly . . . a man you'd see stretched the half of the day in the brown ferns with his belly to the sun"; and in those solitary days in Meath Christy found solace and stay in a wise passivity, in introspection and the building of fancies, and in contact with animals and the natural world.

Appropriately enough an important characteristic of the play is a concern with matters of language. Pegeen praises Marcus Quin for his skill in telling "stories of Holy Ireland"; and the chief delights of Jimmy's life have been "Dan Davies's circus and the holy missioners making sermons on the villainy of man"; they speak of the "preaching North"; there is to be "great blabbing at the wake"; Pegeen presumes that Christy "had much talk and streeleen" on his journey; Christy sees his father as a monster "who'd be raging all times, the while he was waking, like a gaudy officer you'd hear swearing and cursing and damning oaths"; one of the joys Widow Quin promises Christy is to "hear the penny poets singing in an August Fair"; Christy thinks "this'd be a fine place to be my whole life talking out with swearing Christians"; the girls are in ecstasies at hearing Christy's "grand story, and he tells it lovely"; Shawn is despised largely because he has no fluency of speech, he says, "I'm a poor scholar with middling faculties to coin a lie," and so he has to descend to telling the truth; Old Mahon is after walking long scores of miles "winning clean beds and the fill of his belly four times in the day" merely by telling stories of how his son struck him; Old Mahon drunk was "a terrible and fearful case . . . screeching in a straightened waistcoat, with seven doctors writing out his sayings in a printed book"; Pegeen thinks it would be a bitter thing to marry Shawn, and "he a middling kind of scarecrow, with no savagery or fine words in him at all"; Michael James looks forward to "seeing a score of grandsons growing up little gallant swearers"; and it is Christy's words more than anything else that win Pegeen—to her he is a coaxing fellow, he has no match for "eloquence or talk at all," and at the height of their joy in the love-duet they think of happiness in terms of speech: they intend to talk in the spring, to coin "funny nicknames for the stars of night" and they are delighted to know that they are speaking with love and kindness to each other—the climax of the duet is:

> CHRISTY: And to think I'm long years hearing women
> talking that talk to all bloody fools, and this the
> first time I've heard the like of your voice talking
> sweetly for my own delight.
> PEGEEN: And to think it's me is talking sweetly, and I the
> fright of seven townlands for my biting tongue

The above quotations give some notion of the distinctive vitality of the play; it possesses a rich joy that has been rare in our drama since the early seventeenth century, and an abundance of sheer fun to which it is impossible to do justice in the course of this, or of any, exposition. Although its high worth is generally recognized, it is not so often noticed how a good deal of this magnificence comes from an exceedingly skilful use of one or two simple devices. For instance the device of dramatic contrast is used throughout with infinite variety and resource. Synge's skill in this is derived to a considerable extent from his study of earlier dramatists, especially the French, as V. S. Pritchett recognizes.

> To his handling of roguery, Synge brought all the subtlety
> he had learned from Molière . . . it stands out a mile in his

handling of the dramatist's use of continual contrast, whereby almost every speech creates a new situation or farcically reverses its predecessor.

A detailed examination of *The Playboy* would show how true this is, and how there is an unbroken movement from beginning to end, in which each phrase or action blends in, or contrasts with, what has gone before or is to come. There are peaks in the play, but they are parts of a coherent structure, not isolated volcanoes. Or, to vary the metaphor, the development of Christy from weakling to hero is a wave-like movement, an undulation with steep troughs, and the last and greatest wave, lifting him from the bottom of the deepest trough, throws up the new man. At first Christy, worn and anxious, is in a trough. He is lifted from this by the admiration of Pegeen and the villagers. He falls, momentarily, into a shallow trough when Widow Quin hammers on the door, but is carried up on another wave by the sight of two handsome women fighting for his company. He is borne up higher on this wave by the hero worship of Widow Quin and the village girls but Pegeen's anger at this topples him into a steep trough and he experiences a new depth of distress. But, by this time, under the influence of all this stimulation his imagination is becoming more powerful, and his words convince Pegeen that he is truly in love with her, and she receives him back into favour. At once he mounts higher than ever on another wave. His triumph over Shawn and his natty appearance in Shawn's clothes send him even higher, but the unexpected appearance of his father dashes him into a deep trough. Widow Quin helps him out of this, and his singular success at the sports sends him to new heights on another wave. With his love-duet with Pegeen and Michael James's consent to their marriage he soars on this wave to heights of joy undreamed of, only to fall abysmally to the extremest depth of distress when Old Mahon returns. In this final extremity there is no one to help him up: Pegeen and the villagers assail him, and all seems lost. But his imagination is now fully active and potent and his character developed remarkably. And so, stimulated further by Pegeen's hostility, he rises again, and soars up on the final wave beyond the ken of the villagers to a level where his new, superior personality will have scope for action.

To this theme and rhythm the comedy of the play is integral: one remarks, for instance, how Christy's sudden descents from the top of a wave to the bottom of a trough—which are very funny—always occur when he is boasting of his heroism in felling his dad. In fact there are few comedies so well made, few in which humour is so cunningly built into the whole situation that it is not dependent upon the talent of an outstanding comic actor, and hardly requires any "gagging" or stage "business" manufactured by a producer. Clearly in *The Playboy* we have the unusual phenomenon of a play which obeys the rules of twentieth-century naturalism and yet produces a fullness of effect hitherto obtained only by dramatists working in conventions more suitable for the poetic dramatist.

Alongside dramatic contrast there is much irony in the play. It is ironic that as Pegeen's admiration for Christy impelled him to make himself like the image, so her loathing at the end was a big factor in making the transformation complete. Likewise Pegeen believes in the dream, that is, she deludes herself during most of the play, but when the dream becomes actual she rejects it and takes up another delusion—that Christy is "a crazy liar." Ironically enough, Pegeen, the villagers in *The Playboy* and the villagers in *The Well of the Saints* are considered to be "sensible, practical people" in contrast to the more imaginative figures who are thought to be "queer"; yet there is no doubt that Martin and Christy have a much firmer grasp of reality than anyone else has: in all this how exact a reflection of life these plays are. It is ironic too that throughout *The Playboy* there is almost continual talk about stirring deeds and mighty sensations, things or people easily become "wonders," everything is coloured and made to appear more startling and momentous than normal; yet really there is very little action, except for the sports (off-stage) and the scuffle at the end, and to the impartial observer all the objects used or referred to would appear most prosaic. In presenting this immense deal of talk (all of it much more than tolerable) to one poor ha'p'orth of action Synge may have intended, among other things, to have a sly grin at blather and blarney, at the Irish fondness for "a good crack" and verbal virtuosity, at those who manipulate words for their own benefit and others' entertainment—at himself. For *The Playboy* is not devoid of the kind of wit described by T. S. Eliot, which "involves, probably, a recognition, implicit in the expression of every experience, of other kinds of experience which are possible." *The Playboy* displays this kind of tolerance and humanity throughout; it implies a sanity and "a darling freshness deep down things": all the references to the natural world show Nature, benign and sunny, cooperating with Man. These are the dominant effects and tones of a serious and wholesome play which embodies a mature enjoyment of life in many aspects; it is the only work of Synge's in which mutability is not stressed; perhaps because in this play imagination has made an eternal triumph over harsh actuality and time.

A Hard Birth

Donna Gerstenberger

I. Growth of the Play

Of all Synge's plays, *The Playboy of the Western World* has called forth the most persistently uncomfortable reactions from audiences and critics alike, from the date of its first performance in the Abbey Theatre in 1907 to the present time. The underlying cause of the discomfort attendant upon the experience of this play is beginning to be understood by modern readers with the aid of Freud and Frazer. But the *whole* cause is to be explained only by an understanding of Synge's use of the dramatic dimensions and expectations of his material, for the reaction the play arouses is nearly always one of personal outrage, one not wholly to be explained by the Freudian contexts of the play. Reaction to the play differs from that the reader has, for example, to *Oedipus the King* or to *The Brothers Karamazov,* the latter work, in particular, having many parallels with the material of *The Playboy of the Western World.*

Something different happens in Synge's play, and his success in affronting his readers' complacency in *The Playboy of the Western World* is to be explained both in terms of the material of the play and of its artistic accomplishment, the skill with which Synge turns the dramatic mode into an instrument for the audience's recognition. The result of this fusion of method and material is the creation of the play which is generally acknowledged as Synge's masterpiece, at the same time that it is criticized for being an anticlimactic and gratuitously brutal masterpiece.

From *John Millington Synge*. © 1964 by Twayne Publishers, Inc.

The story of the play, the core of which Synge heard in the Aran Islands, is deceptively simple. It involves the arrival of a young man—shy, footsore, and afraid—in an isolated country shebeen (public house) on the coast of Mayo. The information the young man is goaded into giving, that he has killed his father with a loy while digging potatoes, takes on heroic trappings in the eyes of the country men; and, through their reception of him as a hero, the young man, Christy Mahon, is so transformed that when his father arrives, bloody but unbowed, he is quite ready to kill the old man a second and, if necessary, a third time. The inhabitants of the place are not willing to countenance the deed when it is performed in their own backyard, however, and Christy leaves, driving his father before him. Only Pegeen Mike, the girl whose heart Christy has won, has some sense of the desolation which must follow in a world which has been, however briefly, inhabited by such a Playboy.

The care Synge took to make the material of his *Playboy* into a significant dramatic experience has been documented by David Greene, with the result that Synge's concern to control the artistic embodiment of his story is readily evident. Seven years of work went into the transformation of the Aran story into *The Playboy of the Western World,* and he produced at least "ten complete drafts of the play, each one written over and corrected until it had become almost illegible." The third act, according to George Moore in *Hail and Farewell!,* had been rewritten thirteen times.

An early sketch of the play which Synge had recorded in his notebook was called "The Murderer." Act 1, which was to be set in the potato garden, had for its principal action a description of Christy's life by his father, whose contemptuous telling so angered the young man that he hit his father with his loy and ran away. For this version, Synge intended to stage act 2 in a public house with Christy, in control of his audience, telling his boasting story, full of rant and great deeds. The third act was to climax in Christy's election to public office in spite of the appearance of the old man, himself as proud as his son of his broken head. Christy's reversion to cowardice is a significant part of the earlier conclusions of the play, with his deed surviving only in the world of the imagination and unrealized in any objective or meaningful way. Synge's changing conception of the meaning of his material is reflected in the successive working titles for the play, "The Fool of Farnham" and "Murder Will Out," which suggest realizations much more limited than that represented by Synge's final choice.

The earlier versions of the play and the changes which Synge made become an index by which his accomplishment may be measured. In the creation of *The Playboy of the Western World,* Synge learned a great deal from the practical requirements of the small size of the Abbey Theatre stage, which could not accommodate his vision of a plowed field. Synge was faced with the necessity for shifting the scene of his play indoors, a move which underwrote the most important change in the final version of the play. Instead of presenting the audience with the multiple scenes of the first version, Synge came to realize that the real scene of the play is, finally, Christy's imagination, just as the real action of the play is, finally, the growth of his conception of self. That the audience should see the occurrence in the plowed field through Christy's telling and through the reaction of his hearers brings what had originally been exposition into focus as an important and meaningful part of the action of the play. The unrelieved scene of the shebeen becomes itself an unstated motive for much that happens, and a continuous view of the interior of the country public house becomes a source of contrast and tension in the play as the audience sees the world of imagination at work upon the stage.

Synge's own comments about *The Playboy of the Western World* are very helpful in explaining what he was trying to do, although these are a part of his larger concern for the state of drama in his time. Actually, Synge left little behind him by way of explicit, formal dramatic criticism, except the two prefaces, each a brief but concise statement of Synge's intentions in his dramatic work. The preface to *The Playboy of the Western World* is a masterpiece of terse statement, the more remarkable for its contrast to the bountiful, sheer exuberance of speech in the play that it introduces.

In his preface Synge insists that he uses in the play the real speech of a real people he has known from firsthand experience. Synge's insistence in this matter is partly in answer to those critics who had questioned the Anglo-Irish idiom of his earlier characters. Unfortunately, Synge's detailed account of learning to write the speech of the people by listening through a chink in the floor to the conversations of servant girls in a Wicklow kitchen brought new criticism upon the playwright and provided his enemies with the image of the prurient eavesdropper intruding upon the privacy of family servants.

Yet, Synge's assertion of the existence of actual sources for the language of his characters was also, and more importantly, a corollary to his definition of art as "a collaboration." "All art is a collaboration" in the sense that the artist reflects the life of his time and place, for he gives substance and life to his work in terms of the world available to him. Therefore, a widespread loss of vitality in contemporary urban life seemed to Synge (as it did to Yeats) an ample explanation of the dreary work of Ibsen and Zola, in which the "reality of life" must be, by definition, dealt with "in joyless and pallid words." Given the modern urban situation, the only other possibility seemed to be an equally unsatisfactory literature; one which had divorced itself from "the profound and common interests of life"—the literature of the Symbolists.

Synge as a "collaborator" in the Ireland of his time felt himself fortunate, for the language of the people was yet strong and imaginative: "in countries where the imagination of the people, and the language they use, is rich and living, it is possible for a writer to be rich and copious in his words, and at the same time to give the reality, which is the root of all poetry, in a comprehensive and natural form." A rich language, a living idiom, a fertile imagination are a part of the actuality of the world Synge portrays; and they make possible, by *The Playboy of the Western World,* his demand that "on the stage one must have reality, and one must have joy."

By *joy* Synge means life-espousing vitality, the assertion of the creative self, and expressive pleasure in speech and gesture to give form to the other two. And this "rich joy" can be "found only in what is superb and wild in reality." The attempt to present "reality" without "joy" in the theater of ideas or in the Naturalistic theater of the 1890s seemed as much a failure to Synge as it did to Yeats, and both men knew themselves to be more fortunate than those "writers in places where the springtime of the local life has been forgotten, and the harvest is a memory only." This theater which Synge celebrates in his preface is one in which words and gestures of personality are of primary importance, in which the assertion of the creative self becomes the substance of the play, and one which shares with the Elizabethan stage a common source of vitality.

II. Growth of the Playboy

Synge's general theories in his preface provide an appropriate

preparation for the play it precedes, for the discovery and the fulfillment of self on the part of the hero of *The Playboy of the Western World*
are the principal actions of Synge's play. Christopher Mahon, the
self-styled father-killer, creates himself to match the image held up
for him by the excitement-starved imaginations of the country people, and the mirror itself becomes a metaphor for explaining what
happens to the young man in the play. The image of himself which
Christy brings with him from the past was one reflected in "the
divil's own mirror we had beyond, would twist a squint across an
angel's brow." It is the image of the man repressed by the father, who
is himself a raging "divil" of a man; and the image Christy sees in the
father's mirror is that of "Mahon's looney," "the laughing joke of
every female woman where the four baronies meet."

The shy, frightened Christy Mahon who first enters the shebeen
of Michael James is closer in action and character to Shawn Keogh,
his dramatic foil, than to the Playboy he is to become. He is the son
repressed by the father—like Shawn Keogh, who defers to Father
Reilly and the Church in all things and abandons manhood and its
responsibilities in the face of danger: "I'd liefer live a bachelor, sim-
mering in passions to the end of time, than face a lepping savage the
like of him." The recognition of self involves the assumption of manhood, and although the instinctive blow with the loy is the action
which has shattered the facts of the image of the past, it is not until
Pegeen Mike and the others hold up the glass of imagination for
Christy that he begins to grow into the image of self which is the
logical consequence of the "death" of the father and the normal, now
unstinted growth of the son. Although his action had been intuitive,
Christy, as both he and his deed grow with each telling of the tale,
comes to speak of the moment as an epiphany: "(*Impressively*) With
that the sun came out between the cloud and the hill, and it shining
green in my face. 'God have mercy on your soul,' says he, lifting a
scythe. 'Or on your own,' says I, raising the loy."

The old man, it might be worth noting, threatens Christy's
youth with the traditional symbol of time and age, the scythe; and
this is only one of the many symbols and metaphoric patterns which
Synge develops in this play. Not the least of these is a rather extensive
use of clothing in metaphorical terms, a use for which Synge has the
sanction of a long tradition in literature. An example of the way in
which the clothing metaphor works in the statement of *The Playboy*
may be seen in Shawn Keogh's loss of his coat as he seeks to escape

the duties of manhood, the defense of his betrothed in the first act. In the second act, Shawn tries to bribe the Playboy to abandon the field of sexual battle by offering him a fine suit of clothes, and Christy, in newfound arrogance, assumes Shawn Keogh's clothing as he usurps Shawn's prerogatives with Pegeen Mike.

The rage which had driven Christopher Mahon to strike out against his father had itself been the result of a threat to his manhood, for his father had wished to wed him to the Widow Casey, "A walking terror from beyond the hills, and she two score and five years," the woman who had suckled Christy as an infant. After the boy becomes the man, asserting and choosing for himself, capable of winning the hand of Pegeen Mike, his transformation is so complete that he becomes unrecognizable to his father: "That man marrying a decent and a moneyed girl? Is it mad yous are?" The contrast between the man who was and the man who is, is underlined with dramatic effectiveness in the interchanges in which old Mahon pictures the Christy he has known and the man he hears described in Mayo; old Mahon is simply unable to reconcile his early image of his son with that of the Playboy of the Western World. As Christy himself confides to Pegeen, "Up to the day I killed my father, there wasn't a person in Ireland knew the kind I was."

Equally effective (and more moving than comic) is Christy's own emerging recognition of self, which begins tentatively with the telling of his deed and its delighted reception by the people in the shebeen. It is Pegeen Mike, however, who appropriately gives him the image to which he commits himself, for she evokes his first delighted response, "Is it me?" when she speaks of him as a "fine, handsome, young fellow with a noble brow." The extent of Christy's recognition and fulfillment of the self's potential is acknowledged by a repetition of his question in the closing lines of the play. Old Mahon, recognizing the reversal that has taken place in their roles and that he must now play the heathen slave to his son's gallant captain, echoes with equal surprise his son's "Is it me?" The natural cycle has been fulfilled, for the father must give way before the son. The king is dead; long live the king.

The major action of the play, the recognition of self, demands the second "murder" of the old man by the son; but this element in the play receives the almost unanimous censure of critics who regard it as anticlimactic, brutal, and prodigal. The second "murder" is necessary, however, as an index of Christy's transformation; for the first "murder" was intuitive and meaningless to him until it was reflected and magnified in the eyes of the people of the isolated public house. The import of the "murder" in the potato field has grown in Christy's imagination as he improves the event with each recital, beginning simply with the facts and moving, with encouragement, toward the creation of an epic deed of fully heroic proportions. As the man and poet sleeping within him are released, he begins to realize the implications that the deed suggests about its doer.

The Christy who has become the Playboy of the Western World at the games is momentarily thrown back into "shy terror" at the confrontation with his father in the last act of the play; but, upon discovering that he is as alone as every traditional hero must be at the moment of confrontation, he remembers the image of self that has been created and acts accordingly, thus giving objective existence to what had first found life only in the imagination. Although he had been completely subdued at the first sight of his father and willing, in the second act, to hide behind Widow Quin's skirts, his regression is brief in the last moments of the play; he recovers himself so that he may commit, in full consciousness and knowledge, the ritual deed upon which realization of self has been (falsely) founded. This time there will be no lie about burying the father among his spuds; fresh from his gory deed Christy intends to confront Pegeen, who will once again, he believes, give him "praises the same as in the hours gone by." He refuses now, literally and symbolically (in keeping with the pattern of meaning in the clothing metaphor in the play), to hide behind the petticoat the Widow Quin offers him as a disguise for escape. His manhood has been consciously asserted against the oppression of his father, and he will stand without disguise in the confidence of the fulfilled self.

The play takes another turn at this point, however, and Christy is forced to realize that in the eyes of Pegeen and the others "there's a great gap between a gallous story and a dirty deed." His isolation is complete now. "What did I want crawling forward to scorch my understanding of her flaming brow?" asks Christy upon Pegeen's rejection. Without the support of Pegeen, for whose approval he has struck his father a second time, Christy's image of self must fall or stand on its own merits; and the knowledge that the realized self is of inestimable and intrinsic value gives to Christy a strange exultation, which pervades his every speech in the conclusion of the play. This sense of exultation turns his first reaction of horror at the loss of

Pegeen (who has failed to grow into his image of her) into victorious strength, and Synge's directions for Christy's words indicate that, although he is facing immediate torture and eventual hanging, he speaks gaily, delighted with himself. And when he sees his hardheaded father again, there is no longer a momentary fright: "Are you coming to be killed a third time?"

Christy's exultation partakes of that ordinarily associated with the tragic hero, and much in the play suggests the tragic instead of the comic pattern. The recognition of self, the acceptance of manhood and its responsibilities belong to recognizable patterns of tragic action. The comic pattern, which deflates, which neutralizes the inflated humor of the individual, is not observed in the play, except in the case of old Mahon, who is made to acknowledge the natural operation of the life process. It is not the main character of the play who is made to conform to society, however; he fulfills himself, enacts the finally isolated drama of the heroic individual, and leaves behind him the unsatisfactory society of the Western World. The primary aspects of traditional comedy on the stage (which draws man as smaller than life, ridiculous in his pursuit of some inflated notion, and reconciled at last to the necessities of society) are not present in the end of the play, and Una Ellis-Fermor is quite right in her observation that the play is a kind of tragicomedy.

As long as a great disparity exists between Christy and the image he and the country men create of the man "who killed his da," Synge exploits a wonderful and rich source for comedy—a traditional source, indeed, which rises out of the gap between what a man believes himself to be and what he is. This pure comedy finds its climax, symbolic and actual, in the games upon the sand. Christy Mahon, who has projected himself as a father-killer of epic proportions, participates in games which parody, perhaps, the epic games of traditional heroes. He finds that the self created in imagination can triumph in actual contest; released by his vision, he is "astride the moon," "the young gaffer who'd capsize the stars." From his triumph comes the courage to speak to Pegeen Mike of love, and Christy has attained the penultimate stage of his growth. As the gap between the realized and the ideal begins to close, however, the play ceases to be recognizable comedy; and by the end of the play, the result is the kind of recognition usually reserved for tragedy, but one without the fatal consequences attendant upon the tragic genre.

There is no death in the play except that of "Mahon's looney" and of Pegeen's brief hopes.

Knowledge comes not only to Christy Mahon, but at last also to Pegeen Mike, who has become the victim of her own failure of imagination. There is a tragic recognition in her final cry, "I've lost the only Playboy of the Western World." All the excitement of the Playboy has made no change in the small world on the "wild coast of Mayo"; the transformation has been in the character of Christy Mahon, and his departure leaves only Pegeen Mike more painfully aware than ever of the poor and unaltered quality of the life before her, a life in which she had once been willing to accept Shawn Keogh as a good "bargain," there being none better. She has helped to create the Playboy; but, confronted by deed instead of dream, she denies the man who fulfills the image she has held up to his delighted gaze. It is the poet she had loved and not the murderer, and she fails to realize that the one is released by the other, that the murder of the father is, paradoxically, a lifegiving act. Pegeen Mike, who belongs to the limited and materialistic world of the shebeen, cannot follow Christy in all the implications of his blow against oppression. Pegeen's limitations are established in the opening scene in which she orders with evident relish the fine things for her wedding to Shawn Keogh; yet, when the prospective groom enters, she will not even look up from her work to see the man himself. Pegeen Mike is like Nora Burke at first, believing that a "good bargain" makes a good marriage. Shawn Keogh with all his property is an effective contrast to Christy Mahon, who has nothing to begin with but the possibilities of his imagination and the subsequent growth of self-realization. At the crucial moment, however, Pegeen is so firmly wedded to the world of Shawn Keogh that she abandons Christy and cannot hear his repeated plea to see him now as the man he has become and not the man who lied about burying his father in a faraway field.

One of the ironies of *The Playboy of the Western World* is that the Playboy himself must quit "the Western World," having become so much more than the Playboy of the Western World; and a large part of this growth is symbolized by the release of the sleeping poet within Christy Mahon, who first discovers his poetic powers in the telling of his story of murder, in the elevation of a hero that he discovers, with something of surprise, to be himself. He is, as J. B. Yeats, the poet's father, observes, "a young poet in the supreme difficulty of getting born." Christy fulfills his poet's role most clearly in his love duet with Pegeen Mike, who for all her lifelong habit of imagining a fine and brave life unlike the dullness she has known, is second best at fine talk with Christy Mahon, who would "feel a kind of pity for the Lord God of all ages sitting lonesome in his golden chair." The heart *is* a wonder, as Pegeen Mike discovers momentarily; it tames her sharp tongue, but, more important, it has created a man very different from the "quiet, simple poor fellow" Christy once had been. And the finality of the change is evidenced in the fact that Christy, at the close of the play, bound and rejected, is still the poet: "If I do lay my hands on you, it's the way you'll be at the fall of night, hanging as a scarecrow for the fowls of hell. Ah, you'll have a gallous jaunt I'm saying, coaching out through Limbo with my father's ghost." His imagination does not fail him, either, when he bites Shawn Keogh's leg (another action often criticized as unnecessarily brutal). For, by so doing, he states in the only way available to him his refusal to become again the terrified man he had been at the opening of the play, and he takes a delight in mocking Shawn Keogh's perpetual terror in his contempt for a state he has now outgrown.

The power of this play grows, in part, out of the Oedipal situation which it invokes and the ritual murder which it involves. The first "murder" of the father is not viewed with traditional revulsion by the other characters of the play because, as one critic explains, it is akin to the ritual murder of the fairy tale, wherein the convention of the tale itself absolves the act of bloodletting of real horror; indeed, "the themes, the language, the import of the play resemble those of folk tale and myth."

There is another and important element which enters into an explanation of the attitude toward murder in the play. In a very real sense, old Mahon "deserves" to die because he has sought, in his treatment of his son, to thwart the natural process, the cycle of growth and supersession of the father by the son. Pegeen's words to Christy that "it's near time a fine lad like you should have your good share of the earth" acknowledge Christy's right of assertion. Old Mahon's refusal to yield to necessity and to change violates the natural pattern of existence, the same pattern explored by Synge in the lives of the Aran Islanders. The old man is so intent on imposing his will upon life that he proposes to violate the most vital and meaningful natural pattern. Christy's father intends to wed his son to an ancient widow so that he may partake of the comforts of her home without assuming proper responsibility. He relegates his son to the level of a sexual surrogate; he intends to appropriate the use and fruits of Christy's manhood, and the initial rebellion in the boy is one which is both natural and right, one which seeks to restore the proper order of nature. Christy's action has the sanction of a natural process enacted by ritual among primitive peoples, a ritual which may involve the actual death of the superseded priest or father-image.

As Synge insisted to critics of *The Playboy of the Western World,* the story came to him as the record of a real event, which he heard about in the Aran Islands, where he was told of "a Connaught man who killed his father with the blow of a spade when he was in passion, and then fled to this island and threw himself on the mercy of some of the natives." Sheltered from the police by the inhabitants of the island, the man was finally shipped to America; and, although Synge's triumph in *The Playboy* is in his own creation of the character and meaning of the man who killed his father, something of the attitude of the people toward the murder remains. The people can understand, according to *The Aran Islands,* a passionate action and its consequences; their reaction is the feeling of a primitive people "who are never criminals yet always capable of crime, that a man will not do wrong unless he is under the influence of a passion which is as irresponsible as a storm on the sea." Indeed, "Would any one kill his father if he was able to help it?"

III. Complications and Conventions

The horror of the people at the dispassionate second "killing" of the father in *The Playboy of the Western World* is a logical result of this attitude, and it is at this point that the complications in the making of Synge's play are drawn tight, not only on the level of plot but also on that of what is happening to the play itself. What might have been a play with a conventional happy ending—a wedding and a reconciliation—turns instead toward a deeper commitment, the implications of Christy Mahon's discovery of self. The necessity for the second "murder" is beyond the comprehension of the people of Mayo, who are—Synge would seem to say by his changing of the original geographical location of the story he heard in and about the Aran Islands—of the small landowning class, the class of Dan Burke, with all its limitations. The matter of conventional oppression is one the people can understand, and this is usually an oppression identified with the law (the rule of the English), as evidenced by the many references in the play to the "jailor and the turnkey" of Michael James's song: "There we lay bewailing / All in prison bound." Old Mahon's oppression is even more basic, however, than that of the English, for it is based upon the suppression of manhood and a violation of the sanctity of the personality. The Mayo countrymen can understand a reasoned blow against an abstract oppression like that represented by the peelers; they can even accept secondhand a blow against the father in a distant field, but a murder under their very eyes becomes another matter, and they bring all their righteousness to bear on what formerly they had praised.

J. B. Yeats in his essay "Synge and the Irish" claims that no one really believes Christy has murdered his father even the first time, that his hearers merely see before them a young man with a grand capacity for fantasy. Whether or not the Mayo men actually believe Christy is not of major importance, though, for their response to the second action would be the same in any case. Their reception of the first "murder" which Christy reports to them is a response which belongs to the very conventions of the stage world of comedy, a world in which blood is never real blood and deserved blows never really hurt or maim. Instead, such blows become merely symbolic, devoid of any real sense of human suffering, for that kind of pain is not the business of comedy.

When Synge insists upon the "dirty deed" (convincingly reported by the ever-skeptical Philly), he turns his comment against the inhumanity of the hero-worshiping crowd in the shebeen, and, by implication also, against the audience which becomes uncomfortably aware that it too has been willing to accept the murder of the father as long as it was distanced by the comfortable conventions of comedy. The inhuman, humanity-denying reactions to Christy's story of the murder have been precisely those always involved in the acceptance of sensationalism of any kind; and one of the paradoxes of the play lies in the fact that out of such a reaction could grow Christy's awareness of self, the most meaningful kind of human development.

When it is understood that Synge questions the comic mode itself, as indeed he does in all his "comedies," one part of the discomfort his plays have caused to critics and audiences alike is, perhaps, explained. This questioning of the assumptions which make the comic mode possible is Synge's intention in the scene in which Christy is tied to the table and burned by a glowing sod. This action, again, is not gratuitous brutality on Synge's part; instead, the torture of Christy becomes an action objectifying the cruelty latent in "normal" humanity. The people seek revenge on the Playboy for having tricked them into believing in him (in fact, into creating him to believe in) and for having violated (comic) propriety in the enactment of patricide under their very noses. They have, of course, duped themselves in their inability to comprehend, in the first place, the human proportions of the deed Christy proclaims; and when, in his innocence, he strikes through the shallowness and hypocrisy of their hero worship, he has shown in them a failure of imaginative sympathy.

The cynicism which can be bred from convention—comic, social, or religious—is demonstrated by the general attitude toward death in the play. The conventional reaction to Kate Cassidy's death (whose burial was sanctified by six men from her wake "stretched out retching speechless on the holy stones") is a source of comment throughout the play. This attitude permits Michael James to berate Christy in mock anger not for killing his father but for depriving them of the opportunity for a wake (itself once a meaningful source of macabre humor): "aren't you a louty schemer to go burying your father unbeknownst when you'd a right to throw him on the crupper of a Kerry mule and drive him westwards, like holy Joseph in the days gone by, the way we could have given him a decent burial, and not have him rotting beyond, and not a Christian drinking a smart drop to the glory of his soul?" This cynicism is affronted, however, by the appearance of the old man and by the second "killing" by the son.

Christy is quite right in understanding that such a world must be left behind; he cannot free them by his actions, but he has succeeded, ironically with their help, in attaining freedom and manhood for himself. In the last scenes of the play, the torture scenes, and in Christy's departure, Synge dramatically questions the assumptions on which society and its conventions are founded. In this questioning lies part of Synge's originality, according to Vivian Mercier in his fine study of *The Irish Comic Tradition:*

> Unlike the class-conscious Gaelic poets and satirists, Synge sympathizes with the underdog and the outcast, be he tramp or tinker, parricide or blind beggar. It is the respectable citizen who is exposed to ridicule in what William Empson would call the "mock-pastoral" genre represented

by . . . [the comedies]. As Albert Cook has so brilliantly demonstrated in *The Dark Voyage and the Golden Mean,* most comic writing, the world over, takes the opposite position, siding with "normal" people and established society against the neurotic, the criminal, and the social outcast.

Christy Mahon takes with him the "joy" of which Synge speaks in his preface. His is a joy based on a capacity for feeling, for joining word and deed. It is the awakened joy of self-realization, which sends the hero out, as in all Synge's comedies, from the false world of conventional society—a world careful, safe, and materialistic, no longer big enough to contain the Playboy in his full growth. This image of society which Synge created in his *Playboy of the Western World* was of lineament familiar enough to the playgoer to cause a shock of recognition from which Synge tears away, in his final act, the comforting cushioning of comic conventions. This shock, together with a web of political and religious causes, real and imaginary, created the "riots" which attended the play in its early years of stage life. (In an inflated gesture appropriate to the linguistic exaggerations of *The Playboy* itself, the disorderly conduct of the Abbey Theatre audiences has gone into stage history under the title of the *Playboy Riots*.)

IV. THE WHOLE ISSUE

Synge, according to a letter written the morning after the riotous opening night, to his fiancée, Molly Allgood (the actress, Maire O'Neill), was not downhearted. He realized that the reaction of the audience proved beyond doubt that he had reached it: "It is better any day to have the row we had last night, than to have your play fizzling out in half-hearted applause." And, tired with the strain of chronic illness and the effort of his new play, he added: "I feel like old Maurya today. 'It's four fine plays I have, though it was a hard birth I had with everyone [sic] of them and they coming to the world.' " This letter is not, it is well to note, one of a broken man, and it is not likely that in any specific way the disturbances attending the reception of *The Playboy* or the unpopular reaction to the play had anything to do with hastening Synge's death as Lady Gregory suggested and as Yeats and the French critic Maurice Bourgeois seemed romantically inclined to believe. The facts are that, just as Keats died of tuberculosis and not of a reviewer's harsh words, so Synge died of cancer, not of the *Playboy* riots.

Yeats, who was acutely aware of the much-touted political implications of *The Playboy* riots, felt that the real causes for the reaction to the play cut much deeper than political loyalties and showed a world afraid of vitality, threatened by Synge's "joy." Envious of all that it feared to admit into existence, of that which it daily hedged against with the aid of social and religious convention, this world is portrayed in Yeats's lines "On Those That Hated 'The Playboy of the Western World,' 1907":

> Once, when midnight smote the air,
> Eunuchs ran through Hell and met
> On every crowded street to stare
> Upon great Juan riding by:
> Even like these to rail and sweat
> Staring upon his sinewy thigh.

Yeats's poem, precise and accurate, is full of restraint when compared to an opening-night review in a Dublin newspaper, which called the play, among other things, an "unmitigated, protracted libel upon Irish peasant men and, worse still upon Irish peasant girlhood. . . . No adequate idea can be given of the barbarous jargon, the elaborate and incessant cursing of these repulsive creatures." The reaction to *The Playboy of the Western World* had not been unexpected by the directors of the Abbey, for their experience with *The Well of the Saints* and other plays had suggested, as Yeats had written to John Quinn in February of 1905, that there would be "a hard fight in Ireland before we get the right for every man to see the world in his own way." In this struggle, Yeats continued, "Synge is invaluable to us because he has that kind of intense narrow personality which necessarily raises the whole issue."

Although William Fay's claim in no way illumines Synge's accomplishment in *The Playboy* and needs to be reconciled with the fact that Synge had already given years of careful work to this play, he states that Synge wrote *The Playboy* in retaliation for an audience which had found *The Well of the Saints* offensive where no offense had been intended. " 'Very well, then,' he [Synge] said to me bitterly one night, 'the next play I write I will make sure will annoy them.' " Fay scented trouble when he first read *The Playboy,* and with his brother Frank spoke to Synge and "begged him to make Pegeen a decent likeable country girl, which she might easily have been without injury to the play, and to take out the torture scene in the last act where the peasants burn Christy" (a request with which some directors and even the director of the film version of the play have complied). As a part of their argument, the Fays referred Synge to "the approved rules of the theatrical game—that, for example, while a note of comedy was admirable for heightening tragedy, the converse was not true." The Fays were right in sensing what Synge had done in his play, but they were wrong in believing that the changes they wished could be made without doing violence to the whole. What Synge had done in *The Playboy* was, in every case, intentional and not accidental.

William Fay, who watched the audience uneasily from the stage on opening night, January 26, 1907, has recorded that the first sign of distress followed the entrance of the Widow Quin, whom the audience disliked at once. Synge's implications that there are, in the eyes of society, murderers *and* murderers apparently hit its mark: the man who killed his "da" with the blow of a loy is heroic material; the woman who killed her husband by hitting "himself with a worn pick, and the rusted poison did corrode his blood the way he never overed it" has committed a "sneaky kind of murder did win small glory with the boys itself."

It was not the word "bloody" which broke up the audience as Fay had anticipated it would; it was "as irreproachable a word as there is in the English dictionary—the decent old-fashioned 'shift' for the traditional under-garment of a woman." When Christy refuses the Widow Quin's offer of disguise and escape, he speaks the line which has become identified with the riots: "It's Pegeen I'm seeking only, and what'd I care if you brought me a drift of chosen females, standing in their shifts itself, maybe, from this place to the eastern world?" The play is, at this point, making its turn upon the comic mode, and the reasons the audience broke up at the word "shift" were probably a good deal more complex than the first-night audience could understand.

Out of all the bad temper surrounding the riots came a long, anonymous poem, "The Blushes of Ireland," which was printed in the *Dublin Evening Mail* and attributed to Susan Mitchell, Æ's secretary. It concludes,

> We'll shriek—we'll faint—we won't be mute
> Until we've forced you to elimi-

nate that vile word, and substitute
 The chaster sh--mmy.

And, look, sir, do not sh--ft your scenes—
 There's scandal aided and abetted.
Let them now virtue intervenes
 Be chemisetted.

Yield Willie! else your day is done,
 Boyles will break out, and health desert you:
The little Fays your doors will shun
 In wounded virtue.

 Irish playwright William Boyle did withdraw his plays from the Abbey company for a time; and, waving the "shift" as his battle flag, Arthur Griffith and Synge's other enemies carried on a newspaper attack full of venom. (The shift seemed particularly appropriate to the cause since it had been used some fifteen years earlier by Parnell's political enemies as the symbol of his adultery.) Audiences made it impossible for the actors on the stage to be heard during the first week's performances, but, although some of them agreed with the audience's verdict, the players courageously went through the motions of *The Playboy,* saving their voices until the night might come when the play could have the hearing that it deserved. With the help of Yeats's speeches to the crowds and the protection of the police, the play ran for the week that had been scheduled, an action which Lady Gregory later described as "a definite fight for freedom from mob censorship." The fight over *The Playboy* was also carried on during the Abbey's tour of the United States in 1911, where riots and objections were raised by groups of Irish-Americans who had become, through their stereotyping of certain aspects of Irish character, almost that caricature, the "stage Irishman," the Abbey was dedicated to fighting. Fortunately, the lawyer John Quinn was numbered among Irish supporters in America, and he gave Lady Gregory and her troupe the help they needed in combating the ignorance and the uprooted but unchanged provincialism they met with in New York and in Philadelphia. It is interesting to note that forty years after the writing of *The Playboy of the Western World,* some of the American audiences of Eugene O'Neill's *A Moon for the Misbegotten* walked out on the play for the same reason—they were of Irish descent.

 George Bernard Shaw, himself something of a transplanted Irishman, took the opportunity of the American reaction to *The Play-*

boy to speak out against the pseudo-Irish psychology involved: "There are not half a dozen real Irishmen in America outside that company of actors! . . . You don't suppose that all these Murphys and Doolans and Donovans and Farrells and Caseys and O'Connells who call themselves by romantic names like the Clan-na-Gael and the like are Irishmen! You know the sort of people I mean. They call Ireland the Old Country." The stage Irishman whom the Irish-American seemed to prefer was in disrepute in Ireland at least: "the stage Irishman of the nineteenth century, generous, drunken, thriftless, with a joke always on his lips and a sentimental tear always in his eye." The new Irishman may have rejected this picture, but he was sensitive in other directions. He felt that *The Playboy of the Western World* was a threat to the picture of responsible Irish manhood, capable of home rule and of self-government.

Synge's refusal to trade an old stereotype for a new had struck deeply in the Irish consciousness, and the kind of truth which the play creates—one which not only avoids stereotypes but also turns against the stereotyped mode of creating reality—succeeds in challenging the reactions of all audiences, Irish or otherwise, and guarantees for the play a place in the history of the modern theater. "The outcry against *The Playboy,*" according to Yeats in "A People's Theatre," "was an outcry against its style, against its way of seeing"—and Yeats's phrase, "its way of seeing" might well be used to identify what we recognize as a particularly "modern" interest of the stage in the twentieth century, as indeed it is of all the arts in our time.

Character and Symbol

Robin Skelton

Synge began writing *The Playboy of the Western World* in September 1904. At first he called it "The Murderer (A Farce)," and his rough scenario told only of the "murder" (act 1), the "murderer's boastings" (act 2), and of his being elected county councillor, only to be faced at his hour of triumph with his "resurrected" father (act 3). In the winter of 1904–5 the plan was expanded to include the Widow Quin, Pegeen, and Shawn. Thereafter the numerous drafts show a continual process of development. The Widow Quin several times appears about to dominate the play and her part has to be readjusted to the demands of the whole. By November 5, 1906, Synge could tell Lady Gregory: "I have only very little now to do to the Playboy to get him *provisionally* finished." On November 8 he was of the opinion that "a little verbal correction is still necessary and one or two structural points may need—I fancy do need—revision." He read Lady Gregory and Yeats the first two acts on November 13, and the third on November 28. On December 31 he handed over acts 1 and 2 to the Abbey, and the third act was handed over a little later. On January 8, 1907, the play went into rehearsal and many cuts were made at this time. The strong language of the play caused anxiety among the cast and the directors. On January 26 the play was performed and, as is well known, the restive audience rose in uproar at the word "shifts" in the third act. In spite of over fifty cuts that had been made during rehearsal, it was clear that the play retained enough vitality to disturb its audience.

The history of this first "Playboy row," and of the other rows in America does not concern us here. The consequence of the rows,

From *The Writings of J. M. Synge.* © 1971 by the Bobbs-Merrill Company, Inc.

however, was that Synge himself was obliged to comment both in public and in private on his own play. In the programme note for the first production he maintained:

> I have used very few words that I have not heard among the country people, or spoken in my own childhood before I could read the newspapers.

After the first-night riot Synge was reported as telling the *Evening Mail* that he had not attempted "to represent Irish life as it is lived," and as saying:

> I wrote the play because it pleased me, and it just happens that I know Irish life best, so I made my methods Irish.

He was reported as calling his play "a comedy, an extravaganza, made to amuse," and saying, "I never bother whether my plots are typically Irish or not; but my methods are typical."

Synge's own account of what he said in that interview is included in a letter to Stephen MacKenna:

> He—the interviewer—got in my way—may the devil bung a cesspool with his skull—and said, "Do you really think, Mr Synge, that if a man did this in Mayo, girls would bring him a pullet?" The next time it was, "Do you think, Mr Synge, they'd bring him eggs?" I lost my poor temper (God forgive me that I didn't wring his neck) and I said, "Oh well, if you like, it's impossible, it's extravagance (how's it spelt?). So is *Don Quixote!*" He hashed up what I said a great [deal] worse than I expected, but I wrote next day politely backing out of all that was in the interview. That's the whole myth. It isn't quite accurate to say, I think, that the thing is a generalization from a simple case. If the idea had occurred to me I could and would just as readily have written the thing as it stands without the Lynchehaun case or the Aran case. The story—in its *essence*—is probable, given the psychic state of the locality. I used the cases afterwards to controvert critics who said it was *impossible*.

The Lynchehaun case and the Aran case are both instances of men being wanted by the police for murder being given sanctuary by the peasants. The letter to MacKenna makes it clear that Synge's claim to naturalistic reporting was, in this case as in others, a defensive response to criticism. The reference to *Don Quixote* is intriguing and worth bearing in mind.

The letter which Synge wrote to the press as a consequence of the interview is also significant. Synge explained:

> "The Playboy of the Western World" is not a play with "a purpose" in the modern sense of the word, but although parts of it are, or are meant to be, extravagant comedy, still a great deal more that is behind it, is perfectly serious when looked at in a certain light. That is often the case, I think, with comedy, and no one is quite sure to-day whether "Shylock" and "Alceste" should be played seriously or not. There are, it may be hinted, several sides to "The Playboy." "Pat," I am glad to notice, has seen some of them in his own way. There may be still others if anyone cares to look for them.

"Pat" was Patrick Kenny, who had seen the play largely as a prophecy of the downfall of an Ireland that was exporting its strongest inhabitants and being emotionally and spiritually debilitated by the institution of arranged and loveless marriages. Another interpretation was offered by the *Evening Mail* reviewer, who thought the play might be an allegory, though he found it too obscure for him. He suggested that "the parricide represents some kind of nation-killer, whom Irish men and Irish women hasten to lionize." Most reviewers, however, took a more naïve line. The *Freeman's Journal* saw the play as an "unmitigated, protracted libel upon Irish peasant men and, worse still upon Irish girlhood," and referred to it as a "squalid, offensive production, incongruously styled a comedy." D. J. O'Donoghue, in a letter to the same paper, said:

> The continuous ferocity of the language, the consistent shamelessness of all the characters (without exception), and the persistent allusions to sacred things make the play even more inexcusable as an extravaganza than as a serious play.

In a letter to M. J. Nolan of February 19, Synge wrote:

> With a great deal of what you say I am most heartily in agreement—as where you see that I wrote the P.B. directly, as a piece of life, without thinking or caring to think,

> whether it was a comedy tragedy or extravaganza, or
> whether it would be held to have, or not to have, a pur-
> pose—also where you speak very accurately and rightly
> about Shakespeare's "mirror." In the same way you see . . .
> that the wildness and, if you will, vices of the Irish peas-
> antry are due, like their extraordinary good points of all
> kinds, to the *richness* of their nature—a thing that is price-
> less beyond words. . . . Whether or not I agree with your
> final interpretation of the whole play is my secret. I fol-
> low Goethe's rule to tell no one what one means in one's
> writings.

If we add together all these public and private comments of Synge we
get a fairly clear notion, not of the precise "meaning" he himself
attached to his play, but of his attitudes towards the play's message
element. Firstly, he insists that the play is credible in terms of actuality, but should not be labelled comedy, tragedy, or extravaganza.
He suggests that there are "several sides" to the play, and, while
calling it "a piece of life," indicates that it does have a meaning or
meanings and is more than a simple piece of entertainment. He clearly indicates the central ambiguity of mood by his reference to Shylock and Alceste, and also, more significantly, by his reference, when
being questioned by a reporter, to *Don Quixote*. Don Quixote is, like
Christy Mahon, a fantasist and an "outsider." He was used by Cervantes to comment upon the vices and absurdities of the society of his
time. He is himself a fool, but ultimately much less of a fool than the
acceptably conventional realists he encounters, for his folly and his
fantasy are supported and dignified by a view of the world which is
obsessively idealistic and chivalrous, whereas the other people lack
any real conviction or vision. Moreover, in several instances, Quixote persuades others to share for a while his fantasy and to see themselves as fair ladies, nobles, and knights, in a world of dragons and
heroism. Sometimes self-consciously, sometimes humorously or
even derisively, they gain through him a sense of the glories that are
gone and of the dignity they no longer feel they possess. Finally,
however, Quixote is most usually rejected, and rides away, accom-
panied by his faithful, awed, yet sceptical Sancho Panza, to find new
wonders and irradiate other commonplaces with the ideal illumina-
tion of his fantasy.

It is not difficult to see Christy Mahon as a Don Quixote figure,
at once saviour and fool, hero and clown, visionary and madman.

The difference is that it is, at least in part, the peasants who create the vision for him. Initially he is only a scared boy, convinced in his simplicity that he has killed his father. Praised and admired for his derring-do, he becomes both a braggart and a visionary, his words elevating the commonplace into such poetry that Pegeen Mike and even the Widow Quin are dazzled by his eloquence. Inspired thus he becomes, in fact, the hero, winning all the prizes at the races, and though finally he falls from grace when his father returns from the dead, he retains at the close of the action that heroic self-confidence which he has been given.

It is at the end of the play, however, that the Quixote element gives way to another, for Christy again "kills" his father and is immediately viewed with horror and both beaten and betrayed.

It is here that Synge's Shylock parallelism applies. As long as Shylock's "bargain" remained a distant threat and a fantasy Bassanio regarded him amiably. When, however, he attempted to perform in reality what had been disregarded when merely imagined, he was not only regarded with horror but condemned for a crime of conspiracy which had previously been tolerated and even jested over. The parallelism is obviously inexact, but points to Synge's understanding the essential part played by that element of the grotesque and brutal which some of his audience condemned. In one of his sketches for the play Synge, as in *The Tinker's Wedding* plan, attached descriptive epithets to each movement and each small episode. The first act he saw as moving from "comedy and locality" through "Molièrian climax of farce," "savoury dialogue," "Poetical," "Rabelaisian" to the final "diminuendo ironical." The second act uses the words "character," "comedy," and "Poetical" to describe its shape. In the third act alone, after Old Mahon and Christy meet face to face, is the word "drama" used. At that point, indeed, the whole play alters its perspective and characters once found endearing are found to be ignorant, vicious and treacherous.

George Moore recognized this shift in the play when he wanted Synge to alter the ending, saying, "Your end is not comedy, it ends on a disagreeable note." Moore found the physical violence at the end most unacceptable.

> The burning of Christy's legs with the coal is quite intolerable and wouldn't be acceptable to any audience— French, German or Russian. The audience doesn't mind what is said, but what is done—the father coming in with his head bandaged with a dangerous make-up.

Moore later recanted, but his letter must have entertained Synge, for surely one of the points made about the Mayo folk is that they don't "mind what is said, but what is done," a point which could only be driven home by the emphasis upon physical actuality provided by the coal incident and the bloody head of Old Mahon actually "killed" in front of them.

It is at this point that the relationship between language and actuality comes into the picture. Throughout the play there has been, to quote D. J. O'Donoghue, "continuous ferocity of language." The action itself, however, only erupts into violence the once, and, as Pegeen Mike says, "there's a great gap between a gallous story and a dirty deed." It is not only the ferocity of the language that is important; it is what O'Donoghue calls "the persistent allusions to sacred things."

That the play constantly uses religious words is obvious enough. The first impression one receives is that the almost indiscriminate appeals to divinity are intended to point to the use of Christian terminology as a medium for imprecation and a vehicle for superstition. The dignity of the references contrasts with the pettiness of their occasion. It is one way to create comic incongruity and show the spiritual decadence of the West, a decadence which has gone so far that, for all the religious verbiage, the only acceptable Redeemer turns out to be a young man who has killed his da in a scuffle, not Christ Messiah but Christy Mahon.

Once the notion of Christy as in some way related to Christ enters the picture, however, it is likely to dominate it. Stanley Sultan, in a well-argued essay, presents a view of Christy as a Promethean figure whose rebellion against his father symbolizes for the Mayo peasants their wish to revolt against the oppressive forces of the Church as represented by "the Holy Father" in Rome and "Father Reilly" nearer at hand. "Stop tormenting me with Father Reilly," cries Pegeen to Shawn, she being the girl most attracted to the heroic view of parricide. Dr Sultan, however, goes on from this to suggest that "the *Playboy* presents a carefully developed analogue to the ministry and crucifixion of Jesus."

At first blush this may seem an extreme view, but once the analogy has been hypothesized a number of details appear to support it. The village girls bring the newly arrived Christy "presents" and announce "Well, you're a marvel! Oh, God bless you! You're the lad surely!" thus parodying the Epiphany. The triumphant entry of Christy into the house after his ride to victory in the sports, applauded by all the crowds, is followed, after a while, by a judgment scene in which the crowd's mood changes. The episode begins when the betrothal of Pegeen and Christy is blessed by Michael:

> . . . so may God and Mary and St Patrick bless
> you, and increase you from this mortal day.
> CHRISTY *and* PEGEEN: Amen, O Lord!

Old Mahon then rushes in and identifies himself. Pegeen is convinced and turns on Christy:

> CHRISTY: You've seen my doings this day, and let you
>   save me from the old man; for why would you be in
>   such a scorch of haste to spur me to destruction now?
> PEGEEN: It's there your treachery is spurring me, till I'm
>   hard set to think you're the one I'm after lacing in my
>   heart strings half-an-hour gone by. (*To Mahon*) Take
>   him on from this, for I think bad the world should
>   see me raging for a Munster liar and the fool of men.
> MAHON: Rise up now to retribution, and come on with me.
> CROWD (*jeeringly*): There's the playboy! There's the lad
>   thought he'd rule the roost in Mayo. Slate him
>   now, Mister.
> CHRISTY (*getting up in shy terror*): What is it drives you to
>   torment me here, when I'd ask the thunders of the
>   might of God to blast me if I ever did hurt to any
>   saving only that one single blow.
> MAHON (*loudly*): If you didn't, you're a poor good-for-
>   nothing, and isn't it by the like of you the sins of
>   the whole world are committed?
> CHRISTY (*raising his hands*): In the name of the Almighty
>   God.

The echoes of the New Testament here are indisputable. In other parts of the play we are reminded of the parable of the Good Samaritan, when the moaning stranger is left to himself "in the gripe of the ditch" by Shawn and Michael. The binding and wounding of Christy echoes the binding and wounding of Christ and his projected hanging recalls the crucifixion. Pegeen's betrayal of him is Judas-like; after offering intense affection she brings him total betrayal. If we see Christy Mahon as a distorted reflection of Christ Messiah, then we can see Father Reilly and the Holy Father and Shawn Keogh as representatives of the Old Testament religion and those Saducees and Pharisees whom Christ opposed. That the hypothesis we posited has some basis is clear enough. Dr Sultan, however, is more emphatic than we might wish. He says:

> What Synge has concretely presented is a mirror-image of the story of Jesus' mission of exhortation to obedience to His Father. And it is this fact which makes the sudden and shocking reversal in the last minutes of the play comprehensible. Like Jesus, when Christy confronts with the true significance of his message those who have followed and praised him, they prepare to have him executed by the standard method used for common criminals. The crucifixion is no less complete and sudden a reversal in a triumphant short earthly career; and it came about precisely because the people would not risk secular and spiritual trouble when the issue arose.

Later in his essay he says:

> It is through his exploitation in *Playboy* of the ministry and crucifixion of Jesus that Synge crystallized the elements of the play into a coherent masterpiece. The analogue both helps to motivate, and articulates precisely the nature of the reciprocal effects of Christy on the people of Mayo and the people on him. Furthermore, the comic action of Christy's glorification and reunion with his father, and the bitter denouement of rejection and betrayal, are not disparate but integral: the Christ analogue simply and eloquently establishes that they are complementary to each other in a single pattern.

The trouble with this view of the *Playboy* is that the Christ analogue is intermittent. We cannot easily avoid believing in the Christy-Christ parallelism at the judgment scene; apart from anything else Old Mahon's rhetorical question, "Isn't it by the like of you the sins of the whole world are committed?" reminds one instantaneously of that Christ who took upon him all the sins of the world. The parallelism with the Good Samaritan story is also extremely obvious.

Nevertheless, we would have to be ludicrously ingenious to find similarly exact counterparts to the love-talk between Christy and Pegeen (should we see her as the Church, the bride of Christ?), to Widow Quin (the temptation in the wilderness?) and to the double "death" of Old Mahon (the Nativity and the Resurrection?). It would be better, perhaps, to consider one or two more fundamental attributes of the play before allowing ingenuity to outdistance reason.

The Playboy of the Western World is, in my definition, a shanachie play. It originated, at least partly, in a story told Synge by Pat Dirane, the shanachie of Inishmaan. If we look at the other stories told Synge by shanachies, especially in the Aran islands, we may be able to get another perspective upon the play.

The first thing that strikes one about the stories, as opposed to the anecdotes, that Synge heard, is their extraordinary richness of echo. Synge himself pointed to this when he related the story of O'Connor to *Cymbeline*, to the *Two Merchants and the Faithful Wife of Ruprecht von Würzburg* and to the *Gesta Romanorum*. Other stories have the same characteristic. A story of Diarmuid parallels that of the Shirt of Nessus. Another long story, that of the widow's son who, having killed a great many flies, thinks himself a hero and goes out into the world, has echoes of several of Grimm's stories, Greek myths, and medieval romances. Indeed, all the stories told Synge on Aran and elsewhere could be analysed as conflations of several older stories, and most of them contain archetypal elements.

If we look at the structure of the *Playboy* in these terms it becomes apparent that it has several characteristics in common both with the shanachie story and the shanachie anecdote. Firstly, the material of the play has been created from many disparate sources. Dr Saddlemyer lists three passages from *The Aran Islands*, twelve from *In Wicklow, West Kerry and Connemara*, and five from various notebooks, and all these, either in language or theme, relate directly to different parts of the play. Moreover, the "Good Samaritan" episode in the *Playboy* relates to the death of Patch Darcy in *In The Shadow of the Glen*; Christy telling us he is "handy with ewes" is reminiscent of the use of that image in the same play, and the "poet's talking" of Christy recalls the "poetry" of the Douls in *The Well of the Saints*. Christy says to Pegeen:

> Let you wait to hear me talking till we're astray in Erris when Good Friday's by, drinking a sup from a well, and making mighty kisses with our wetted mouths, or gaming

> in a gap of sunshine with yourself stretched back unto your
> necklace in the flowers of the earth.

Martin Doul says to Molly Byrne:

> Let you come on now, I'm saying, to the lands of Ivereagh
> and the Reeks of Cork, where you won't set down the
> width of your two feet and not be crushing fine flowers,
> and making sweet smells in the air.

Some of these echoes of earlier writings may have been unconscious,
but Synge's own defensive emphasis upon his play's actuality makes
it clear that he was aware of the conglomerate character of his work.
Moreover, as one looks through the worksheets for the *Playboy* there
are numerous indications of a highly conscious process of gathering,
reconstructing, and paring.

If, then, the *Playboy* is as conglomerate as many of the shanachie
tales in its fusing together of separate events and ascribing them all to
one occasion, does it have other attributes of those tales also?

It is here that the mythic element in the *Playboy* falls into place.
Just as the O'Connor story can be related, at different places, to several older and archetypal stories and legends, so *The Playboy of the
Western World* can, at different times, be related with differing degrees
of precision to the New Testament, to *Don Quixote,* and to stories
current among the folk of the west of Ireland. Synge has, indeed, not
only created a play from shanachie material; he has created a play
which has precisely the same kind of richness as the shanachie material, a play fitfully illuminated by archetypal echoes and allusions,
which, nevertheless, retains coherence, not upon the mythic, but
upon the narrative level. The "psychic state of the locality" is
expressed in a language of such strength that it dominates and unifies
the play. *The Playboy of the Western World* is not allegory or parable or
myth or antimyth. If it must be given a label, the label must be
invented, for the method of construction and the manipulation of
echo and theme are entirely original, and very few other playwrights
have profited by Synge's discoveries. Among these, however, and
obviously, is Sean O'Casey whose mature drama uses the same shifting levels of meaning, the same intermittent symbolist power, and
the same ferocity and lyricism of speech.

This view of the *Playboy* relates it closely to Synge's other work,
and permits us to see that the basic technique of conglomeration
alters little from *When the Moon Has Set* and *The Aran Islands* to the

later work. Nevertheless, just as *The Aran Islands* is, in its symphonic construction of impressions, more than a simple retelling of collected experiences, so the *Playboy,* while being typical of shanachie tales in its manipulation of anecdote and archetype, is much more than an extravaganza. While the plot is simple, the language is not, and the characters act as vehicles for themes of which they themselves are unaware. This is typical of Synge. One cannot suppose that Maurya knew of Hippolitus or Nora Casey of the Widow of Ephesus, any more than one can believe that Martin Doul saw his rebellion against the saint in other than terms of purely private necessity. In all Synge's drama, after *When the Moon Has Set,* where the themes are consciously presented by the hero, the characters embody or exemplify attitudes and principles of universal significance. They are thus, every one of them, to a greater or lesser extent, ironic creations, for they are unaware of their own cosmic significance as exemplars and embodiments, while struggling desperately to achieve lesser dignities. *Deirdre of the Sorrows* is the only exception to this rule. There is pathos in this, as when Martin Doul prefers his physical blindness to the spiritual blindness of the saint and unwittingly epitomizes heroically one aspect of the Protestant ethic and the principle of dissent, and as when Sarah Casey, the embodiment of all culturally rich yet deprived minorities, seeks a respectability less filled with dignity than the individualism of her own tradition.

In the *Playboy,* however, the central character arrives, though confusedly, at an understanding of his own symbolic standing, and thus, at the close of the play, triumphs not only over his rejection by the society that first admired him, but also over the irony which is inherent in all human yearnings after dignity. He is, in some ways, the counterpart to Luasnad who, recognizing the manipulation of the gods, yet, in a moment of tragedy, asserts the presence of individual passion and will. Christy Mahon, displaced, rejected, and bereaved of the object of his love, does not, like Maurya, keen at the mortal lot, like Nora express fear of the freedom rebellion has at last brought, or like Sarah Casey return, with only a modicum of increased awareness, to the life she has previously wished to alter; nor does he, like Martin Doul, face the consequences of his rebellion with a stoic dignity and a dream of romance: he exults in his understanding of his own dionysiac potential, and walks away from Mayo with a yea and not a nay upon his lips.

That Synge, in working out his play, thought in terms of character as much as theme is clearly observable from the worksheets. There are continual changes in speeches, but almost all appear to be made in order to clarify the relationships of the characters and make the development of the plot more credible. There are no crudely symbolist speeches, as there are in the drafts of *The Tinker's Wedding.* Queries and hesitations relate to human encounters rather than to archetypal references, though it is noticeable that in the discarded drafts there are many uses of religious terminology and these increase as the play proceeds. It was, it appears, from a rigorous exploration of "the psychic state of the locality" and of the interrelationship of characters, each a vehicle for attitudes and principles endemic in that locality, that Synge developed the mythic richness which Stanley Sultan sees as a Christian analogue that coheres and dignifies the drama.

If this is the case it might be as well to consider the characters of the play and their functions. It would be interesting, indeed, to do this in depth and to study the way in which each character developed throughout the numerous drafts. This would, however, be a book in itself, and in the present book I am concerned with Synge's creative procedures only in as far as they illuminate the finished work, and with his discarded materials only in so far as they point to aspects of the plays which might otherwise escape detection or be merely suspected and not proven.

It seems reasonable to dispose of some minor characters fairly summarily. Philly O'Cullen and Jimmy Farrell are, like the voices of the crowd, largely used to express collective feeling. Their first major part is played in the cross-examining of Christy where they show something of the "psychic state of the locality." Jimmy establishes Christy's masculinity by thinking he may be being hunted for following "a young woman on a lonesome night." Philly reveals the general attitude to landowners by suggesting that "maybe the land was grabbed from him and he did what any decent man would do." Philly says: "Well that lad's a puzzle-the-world," and Jimmy agrees: "He'd beat Dan Davies' Circus or the holy missioners making sermons on the villainy of man."

Thus Jimmy reveals that the moral content of religion is of less importance to him than its value as entertainment, and that he finds the diatribes of the missionaries as delightfully inexplicable as the feats of the circus performers. Philly gives us crude nationalism in his suggestion that Christy may be one of those who had fought on the Boer side in the war and who were now liable to be "judged to be hanged, quartered and drawn." (An earlier draft of this speech made a more explicit reference to "Major MacBride, God shield him, who's afear'd to put the tip of his nose into Ireland fearing he'd be hanged quartered and drawn.") Both Philly and Jimmy are convinced that Pegeen would be safe with a man like Christy in the house, and that the "peelers" would be afraid of him, and thus indicate the general view of legality as an irrelevance.

In the second act the two men are not present. Their picture of the situation is here enlarged and modified by the four girls Nelly, Sara, Susan, and Honor. (In the first production there were only three girls, Nelly's speeches being given to Honor.) They bring Christy gifts, thus parodying the Epiphany. Sara reveals the kind of heroes they approve of when she says to both Widow Quin (who is reputed to have killed her husband) and Christy:

> You're heroes surely, and let you drink a supeen with your arms linked like the outlandish lovers in the sailor's song. There now. Drink a health to the wonders of the western world, the pirates, preachers, poteen-makers, with the jobbing jockies, parching peelers, and the juries fill their stomachs selling judgments of the English law.

The lumping together of the preachers with the pirates and poteen-makers, and of the peelers with the jockies and bribed juries, indicates the cynical realism as well as the romantic love of wildness and roguery which is characteristic of this western world.

In act 3, Jimmy and Philly act at first as chorus and then as commentators upon the sports on the strand, and bring a touch of the grotesque into the play by their talk of bones and skulls. Philly says:

> When I was a young lad, there was a graveyard beyond the house with the remnants of a man who had thighs as long as your arm. He was a horrid man, I'm telling you, and there was many a fine Sunday I'd put him together for fun, and he with shiny bones you wouldn't meet the like of these days in the cities of the world.

Mahon replies:

> You wouldn't is it? Lay your eyes on that skull, and tell me
> where there was another the like of it, is splintered only
> from the blow of a loy.

Philly's reference may be to one of the ancient Irish heroes. Finn's reputed grave just off the Westport-Murrisk road is on a hill above a farm and is twenty feet long. It may be of this Synge is thinking or of other stories of the stature of the warriors of the past. The result in the play, however, is to establish Christy's deed as comparable to those of the Fianna. Later in this act, Philly and Jimmy and their fellows take part in the binding of Christy after Old Mahon has been "killed" a second time.

Thus Philly and Jimmy and the four girls play chorus and initially help to build up the picture of the mores of the society in which Christy finds himself. Michael's role in the play is scarcely more substantial. He serves to emphasize the cowardice of Shawn Keogh, to underline the bibulous aspect of the society, to parody religious ceremonial in his blessing of Pegeen and Christy, and to lead in the binding of Christy in the third act. It is he, however, that it is better to breed "little gallant swearers" by Christy than "puny weeds" by Shawn Keogh, for all Shawn's wealth.

Shawn Keogh is of most importance at the beginning of the play where he displays his cowardice and his total subservience to the will of the Church. He has no will of his own, wondering if he would have the "right" to visit Pegeen, expressing fear of the dark, showing his selfishness in his running away from the groaning man in the ditch, and telling all that he is "afeard of Father Reilly." Though godfearing he is also treacherous. When Widow Quin tells him:

> It's true all girls are fond of courage and do hate the like of
> you—

he replies:

> Oh, Widow Quin, what'll I be doing now? I'd inform
> again him, but he'd burst from Kilmainham and he'd be
> sure and certain to destroy me. If I wasn't so Godfearing,
> I'd near have courage to come behind him and run a pike
> into his side.

In his attempting to bribe Widow Quin to marry Christy, and in his telling Michael James that if Christy marries Pegeen he will lose the promised "drift of heifers" and the "blue bull from Sneem," he exposes the materialism of the peasants.

It is with Pegeen Mike, the Widow Quin, and Christy Mahon that we should be most concerned. Pegeen Mike differs from the other girls in the energy of her passions, the liveliness of her tongue, and the decisiveness of her temper. Rejecting Shawn Keogh, she also rejects the paternal authoritarianism of the Church, as she, too, pays little heed to the authority of her own father. Attracted by Christy, she uses him to further her search for identity, freedom, and romance, finding his words and his deeds heroic and poetic. When Old Mahon returns to life she is angered by having been fooled. When Old Mahon is killed the second time and Christy set upon and tied, it is she who leads in the tying and it is she who ruthlessly burns him with the lighted turf. Pegeen's intensity of feeling leads her towards both total acceptance and total rejection. Her spirit is akin to the Playboy's in its extreme vitality, and it is this that attracts her to him and also causes her to reject him.

Pegeen contrasts with Widow Quin who, like the village girls, finds Christy attractive, but, unlike Pegeen, does not expect integrity in her hero. She is not too perturbed by the arrival of Old Mahon, and delightedly connives at the suppression of the true facts. She herself wants Christy as her man, but her morality is dubious. She offers him other girls as if she were to be his procuress rather than his bride, and her view of life appears to be totally unprincipled. She is a strong character in the play and dominates most of the action when she is on stage. By her candid self-seeking she reveals the moral confusion of her friends and neighbours. They swear by their God, and take His name in vain. The Widow rarely uses the name of God. Indeed, in the whole play she uses the word only twice. The first occasion is when she tells Christy:

> When you see me contriving in my little gardens, Christy Mahon, you'll swear the Lord God formed me to be living lone and that there isn't my match in Mayo for thatching or mowing or shearing a sheep.

The second is when she says of Pegeen to Christy:

> God help her to be taking you for a wonder, and you a little schemer making up a story you destroyed your da.

Her attitude to the hectic religious language of the others is well shown when Christy asks her to help him win Pegeen.

> CHRISTY: . . . Aid me for to win her, and I'll be asking
> God to stretch a hand to you in the hour of death,
> and lead you short cuts through the Meadows of
> Ease, and up the floor of Heaven to the Footstool
> of the Virgin's Son.
> WIDOW QUIN: There's praying!

The Widow Quin observes the goings-on with a mixture of detached amusement, sympathy, and mischievous opportunism. She sees Christy and Pegeen for what they are.

This, however, is her limitation. For Christy's world is not the real one. It is a world of high words and great claims, and he is so intoxicated and elevated by his dream that he actually makes it come true. He does show himself a leader of men, in that he wins the contests on the sands, as if he were a hero at the Greek games. He is admired by the girls and, even after his downfall, he retains some of their affection. Moreover, while he does not become a father-killer, he does become his father's master. Words have created the reality they pictured. Moreover, he now understands the importance of having a proper conceit of himself, and knowing his dignity as a unique human creature. This has been given him as much by the times of glory as by the hours of defeat. For all his blusterings, his elaborate appeals to the heavenly powers, and his confusions of Christian values, he has discovered something which is more important than Pegeen's belief in the need for integrity, and than Widow Quin's materialist realism, and than Shawn Keogh's submission to his Church. He embodies the wildness, the richness, the idealism, and the romanticism of the West in his own person, and he has found that it is possible to transfigure existence with the poetry of energy and passion.

Rejecting Christy, Pegeen realizes that she has rejected the only one who had the secret of transforming the dullness of life into radiance. She herself made him; she, with her passion for idealism and rebellion, convinced him of his own glory, but then the creation outdistanced the creator who became afraid of the creature she had invented. Pegeen is, after all, no more than a village girl and, at least according to the Widow Quin, not particularly exceptional. Christy, however, is exceptional. He becomes much more than a village hero. He becomes an orphic figure whose music survives his destruction. He becomes, indeed, an immortal, for he sees himself living out a "romping lifetime from this hour to the dawning of the judgment day."

Pegeen is another of Synge's passionate, disturbed women hungry for freedom and romance, and she comes closer to success than her predecessors. Nevertheless, her pride and the fundamental puritanism of her temperament make it impossible for her to accept the consequences of her own dream. She cannot accept the Romancer that is Christy, nor can she face his loss without grief. She represents an Ireland that dreaming of independence cannot accept the consequences of the dream becoming reality any more than that faith in spiritual power to which she gives lip service. For Christy is a representative of faith and spiritual power. He will be "master of all fights from now," because of that faith. Poverty of spirit is the disease Pegeen and all Ireland must recognize.

It is now that the utility of the Christ-Christy analogue can be seen. Christy is a poor man who achieves spiritual authority by pursuing, through times of weakness and despair, a vision of freedom that transfigures his own life and that of the people about him. His betrayal and crucifixion cannot break his spirit. He faces death and hell with courage and gaiety. Betrayed by those who crowned him king, he nevertheless triumphs. A parody of Christ rather than a reflection of Him, he gives the society he enters the exact leader they wish for—one of those whom Pegeen describes when she laments the passing of the great ones of the past such as "Daneen Sullivan knocked the eye from a peeler" and Marcus Quin who told "stories of holy Ireland till he'd have the old women shedding down tears about their feet." Societies get the leaders they deserve and Christy Mahon is more fitted for Mayo than Christ Messiah, but even Christy is betrayed. There is no wonder perhaps that this play aroused many of its more perceptive but oversensitive spectators to fury.

Approaches to *The Playboy*

Nicholas Grene

> The Playboy *is not a play with a "purpose" in the modern sense of the word, but, although parts of it are or are meant to be extravagant comedy, still a great deal that is in it and a great deal more that is behind it is perfectly serious when looked at in a certain light. This is often the case, I think, with comedy, and no one is quite sure today whether Shylock or Alceste should be played seriously or not. There are, it may be hinted, several sides to* The Playboy.

Synge's cautiously worded letter to the *Irish Times,* following the "Playboy riots," is well known. To critics of the play, it reads like a challenge to understand the complexities of a work which the Dublin audiences had so completely failed to comprehend. Synge's "hint" has not been neglected; several sides of *The Playboy* have been thoroughly investigated, and it has been looked at in a number of different lights. The letter, however, still illustrates the peculiar critical problems which the play raises. It is accepted that there are "several sides" to *The Playboy,* but it is hard to avoid stressing one side at the expense of another, difficult to find a critical view which will adequately represent the play's multiplicity. *The Playboy* is accepted as "serious." There it is in all the anthologies of modern drama—no one is likely to dismiss it as a slight extravaganza. The problem indeed is how to handle its seriousness lightly enough, how to interpret a serious play which includes scenes of extravagant comedy. There are moments in *The Playboy* which are extremely funny, outbursts of real hilarious laughter. In the critical search for meaning, there is

From *Synge: A Critical Study of the Plays.* © 1975 by Nicholas Grene. Macmillan, 1975.

always a danger that such moments will be "solemnised" or neglected, and that the life of the play will vanish. Looking over a range of the various critical approaches to *The Playboy,* we can see the difficulty in finding an approach sufficiently flexible to do justice to Synge's constantly changing technique.

One of the most inflexible and unhelpful critical attitudes involves the detection of concealed analogies. Christy Mahon, it has been claimed, is a parody version of Cuchullain—or at least "has done a deed equivalent to Cuchullain's in modern peasant terms." Or Christy the parricide is a mock Oedipus, and the structure of *The Playboy* is matched point for point with *Oedipus Rex.* Even more often the playboy has been seen as a Christ figure. Beginning with the argument that Christy's progress is an analogue for Christ's, a scapegoat who can, however, only save himself and not the world, the theory is elaborated to the point where one critic claims that "it is through his exploitation in *Playboy* of the ministry and crucifixion of Jesus that Synge crystallised the elements of his play into a coherent masterpiece."

What is wrong with this sort of criticism is that it is quite unrelated to the actual experience of *The Playboy.* The action of the play is rooted in a substantial and immediate reality, without mythical or literary *arrière-pensées.* There is no evidence to support the idea that Synge intended to parody any of the figures suggested, Cuchullain, Christ or Oedipus, and this is an argument that needs evidence to support it. It is not a matter of unconscious or semiconscious echoes, where the degree of authorial awareness may be left uncertain. The mock-heroic style implies a deliberate imitation of another structure, in which the consciousness of disparity is all-important. Synge was no Joyce or Eliot. He had not the mind which could see and delight in endless ironic correspondences. The reader of modern literature, his appetite whetted for parody, must be careful not to look for mock-heroics everywhere.

"Synge intended that the play should run its course between antinomies. It is, for all its apparent simplicity of plot, a delicately balanced system of ironies, ambivalences, both of words and situation." It is difficult for critics to avoid upsetting this delicate balance, by leaning on one side or another. For instance, in the attitude which we are supposed to adopt towards the playboy himself, there are two basically opposed views which make up an axis of critical debate. Alan Price remarks that *The Playboy* might be taken as an illustration of Keats's dictum: "The Imagination may be compared to Adam's dream—he awoke and found it truth." He traces the way dream is transformed into actuality and sees the ending of the play as the triumphant vindication of the creative imagination. Una Ellis-Fermor argues that the central movement of the play is the "growth, like a Japanese flower dropped into a bowl of water, of Christopher Mahon's new self." According to Patricia Spacks, Christy through a series of fantasy adventures reaches a peak of real achievement in the dominance of his father and the crowd. For all these critics, Christy is like the romantic poet, a self-created myth-maker.

Such romantic conceptions of *The Playboy*, however, have not gone unchallenged. Howard D. Pearce, for example, questions whether the ending is a real triumph for Christy, and stresses the importance of the Widow Quin's part in the play: "If Widow Quin lacks the sparkle and romance of Christy, nevertheless her actions, grounded in actuality, in such sharp contrast to Christy's, which are irremediably floating in the dream vision, point up Synge's ironic detachment." Ronald Peacock sees another sort of irony at work in the play. He comments on what he calls "Synge's delicate self-mockery" and implies that in *The Playboy* the author is parodying his own attraction to gaudy and outrageous language. R. R. Sanderlin holds that the play is in fact a direct satire on Irish romanticism—on blather and blarney. As the "poetry talk" of all the characters is uniform, and the Mayo men are as poetic as Christy, he argues that they are all equally satirised and that it is unreal to distinguish between the imaginative playboy and the prosaic "fools of earth."

The critical controversy here represents a real ambiguity in the play. Price's analysis, for example, of the peaks and troughs of Christy's self-confidence, his progress to hero-status, is very illuminating. On the other hand, there are scenes which he neglects almost completely, or remarks of them vaguely that they illustrate Synge's capacity for amusing comedy. The emphatic focus on Christy tends to reduce the importance of other characters and other views in the play. For the romantic vision is indeed qualified by irony, and Synge does make us aware of the poetic extravagance of Christy:

> CHRISTY: Amn't I after seeing the love-light of the star of
> knowledge shining from her brow, and hearing words
> would put you thinking on the holy Brigid speaking
> to the infant saints, and now she'll be turning
> again, and speaking hard words to me, like an old
> woman with a spavindy ass she'd have, urging on a hill.

> WIDOW QUIN: There's poetry talk for a girl you'd see
> itching and scratching, and she with a stale stink of
> poteen on her from selling in the shop.

The widow's speech reveals the ironic disparity between the image and the reality, and exposes the hyperbolic nature of Christy's language. But irony is not simply corrosive, it is a controlled and measured effect. We do not dismiss the poetry as "blather and blarney" because it is undercut by the widow's cynical realism. The Widow Quin sees Pegeen by the harsh light of day, in a sense more clearly than Christy can, yet Christy's description of his emotion is vivid and genuine, and in no way denied by the incongruity of object. Negative does not cancel out positive, but between the two an electric current is set flowing.

Those who emphasise the progress of Christy through the play, often press home an identification of the playboy as poet. It has been argued by J. F. Kilroy that "*The Playboy of the Western World* dramatises the gradual development of the poet's craft from its first uncertain expression to the full display of mature art." The prizes presented to Christy after the sports, according to Arthur Ganz, "suggest consecration of a bard rather than triumph as an athlete." Edward Stephens considers that it was his own growth as an artist which Synge symbolised in the play.

It seems likely that Stephens is right, and that *The Playboy* did have its origins in personal experience; it may well be that the unexpected blossoming of the shy and inarticulate Christy somehow represented Synge's own surprising success as a dramatist. But tracing back to the emotional sources of a work does not always supply us with significant truths about it, and to see in *The Playboy* a detailed allegory of the development of the artist is to restrict rather than to enrich its meaning. Christy Mahon is not a poet, in the literal sense, nor can he be said to symbolise the artist as such. There may well be poets like Christy, but there are many Christys who are not poets. He is rather, like the tramps of Wicklow, a "temperament of distinction," a man capable of imaginative reflection. Synge did once attempt an artistic self-portrait in *When the Moon Has Set,* and the result was the effete and pretentious Colum. One of the sources of Christy's lasting attraction is that he is not a writer of prose poems, but a far more basic and complete representative of the imagination.

Literary criticism of drama is always in danger of becoming too exclusively literary, not to say academic. The "portrait of the artist as playboy" is the sort of ingrowing interpretation to which we are prone, transferring the apprehension of the play to a familiar world of intellectual analysis. It is all too easy to reduce a play to the sum of its themes, and lose the sense of its dramatic dimension. Particularly with *The Playboy,* where so much of the effect depends upon variation in dramatic mode, where "several sides" alternate, we must not let ourselves be drawn away from the substance of the play by attractive literary interpretations. Perhaps the best way to approach *The Playboy,* therefore, is to establish the simple theatrical forms on which it is based, and then to look at the way Synge develops them towards something more complex. The technique is similar to that which we have already seen in *The Shadow* and *The Well of the Saints,* but with *The Playboy* it is still more elaborate than in the other two.

The first extant record of *The Playboy* is a scenario entitled "The Murderer: A Farce" in which the action was to begin with the fight between father and son in the potato garden, and to end with Christy's exposure just as he has been elected county councillor in Mayo. It was farce which provided Synge with the basic structure for his play. Its central device is what Bergson called the "snowball"—the preposterous growth of a misconception which we find also in Lady Gregory's little one-act plays, *Spreading the News* and *Hyacinth Halvey.* As so often with farce, it depends on a simple mechanism for the creation of misunderstanding. Indeed, Bergson's theory of comedy, although he ingeniously extends it to the comedy of character and wit, belongs most properly to farce, for there the source of laughter is, as he claims, the substitution of mechanical for vital process. Instead of seeing people behaving normally, that is with an autonomous will subject only to social custom and necessity, we watch them enslaved by an artificial system the operation of which only we, the audience, understand. A comic providence brings all the lovers to the same place of assignation, or contrives that letters should be switched, or brings long-separated identical twins on the scene at the same moment. It is such a mechanism, a mechanism which gathers speed and momentum as the action progresses, that we find in *The Playboy.* The lie expands to such monstrous size that it becomes inevitable that it should be exploded. In early versions of the play, the device was more obviously mechanical, with Christy's steps to glory taking the tangible form of election as county councillor, marriage with Pegeen, appointment to a government sinecure. Synge's instinct, also, was to preserve the circular movement commended by Bergson as the finest type of the "snowball," and in all the first drafts Christy ends up as the snivelling weakling—the "Fool of Farnham"—once again.

The farcical substratum remained in the completed text, where Christy is led on by easy stages to claim that he "cleft his father with one blow to the breeches belt." We watch with delight as the blow, through successive versions of the story, travels down the old man's anatomy. Each new outrage against our sense of truth adds to our feeling that the author is testing the limits of Christy's powers of fantasy and the stage audience's capacity for credulity. As in *Henry IV, Part 1* where Falstaff creates eleven adversaries out of two in the space of some five minutes, we wait expectantly for the balloon to be burst. Christy, in fact, is deflated again and again. In the first act, when he is just beginning to swell with his new sense of pride—"and I a seemly fellow with great strength in me and bravery of"—a knock at the door sends him running to Pegeen in terror: "Oh, glory! it's late for knocking, and this last while I'm in terror of the peelers, and the walking dead." Or again just before the actual arrival of his father, he is boasting of his deed to the Widow Quin.

Christy and Falstaff share as common ancestor the *miles gloriosus* of Roman comedy, and yet Christy is very different from the traditional comic boaster. He is not a knowing, a conscious liar like Falstaff. His lies are not "gross as a mountain, open, palpable," but unconscious fantasies which delicately mark his own growing sense of self-esteem. If much of the comic momentum of the play derives from the successive deflations of Christy the boaster, yet this pattern also expresses a real development in his character. Although in the earliest drafts Synge kept the more usual comic denouement, with the return to status quo ante, the final text shows a definitive change in Christy by the end of the play. There is here a duality which is central to Synge's vision: the playboy as a comic type is by definition incurable, the daydreamer whose fantasies are constantly exposed by reality; and yet the "likely gaffer" of the end has learned by his mistakes, has achieved that development which the dimensions of the comic stock-character seem to preclude.

We can readily believe in Christy's growth. From the beginning he is extremely naïve, and when asked the motive of his crime, he replies disarmingly: "He was a dirty man, God forgive him, and he getting old and crusty, the way I couldn't put up with him at all." Which is no more than the truth, after all. Here, as so often in the play, even the most obviously comic passages help us to establish the reality of Christy's past life with his father. When he is telling the fully elaborated story of the murder in act 2, some of the dialogue he recounts has the unmistakable ring of truth: " 'You squinting idiot,' says he, 'let you walk down and tell the priest you'll wed the Widow Casey in a score of days.' " We are to see very shortly that this is indeed Old Mahon's peremptory style of conversation. The father's account of his son, when he does appear, is comically biased, but it too contributes to our understanding of Christy. Christy, he says, is "a lier on walls, a talker of folly, a man you'd see stretched the half of the day in the brown ferns with his belly to the sun." Mahon intends this as a description of a lazy good-for-nothing, but we may guess that Christy's talk may have had more to it than idle foolishness. Again "he'd be fooling over little birds he had—finches and felts—or making mugs at his own self in the bit of a glass we had hung on the wall." We have already heard from Christy of the "divil's own mirror we had beyond, would twist a squint across an angel's brow," and the corroboration is amusing. But the bird fancying is almost certainly intended to be a mark in Christy's favour. A love for natural things is a sure touchstone of value in Synge. Our sympathy for Christy is engaged even as his pretensions to glory are debunked.

While the myth of the playboy remains static, and Christy tries desperately to live up to it, a real and organic change is taking place in his personality. At the end of act 1 Christy sums up his position: "it's great luck and company I've won me in the end of time—two fine women fighting for the likes of me—, till I'm thinking this night wasn't I a foolish fellow not to kill my father in the years gone by." This is purely comic, the direct address to the audience has the knowingness of farce. But in the second act Pegeen's admiration for Christy becomes more to him than merely an instance of his "great luck and company." Partly because she was the first girl to take an interest in him, partly because he senses in her a special response to his fine words, Pegeen occupies the centre of his mind. The "two fine women" were of more or less equal value, but by the end of act 2 Christy is pleading with Widow Quin: "Aid me for to win Pegeen. It's her only that I'm seeking now." He is in love for the first time, and though his love is still part of the image of the admired playboy, it now has priority over everything else. It earns him our admiration and sympathy, narrows our comic distance from him.

In the final act Christy reaches a new peak of self-assurance as playboy in his triumph at the sports. The "crowning prize," however, is still Pegeen, and when he is discomfited by the appearance of his father, it is her love only which he wishes to regain. He no longer cares for general adulation, but commits the "second murder" so that "Pegeen'll be giving me praises the same as in the hours gone by." The braggart has completely disappeared, and Christy is a young lover like any other desperate to win the approval of his mistress. It is the terrible shock of her betrayal of him which awakes him from his dream. His belief in Pegeen is shattered but this ultimately only strengthens his belief in himself. Where before he had thought his love, and the words he used to express it, originated with her, his inspiration, he can now see that it had springs within himself. The play traces Christy's development from dependence on his father, through dependence on his first love, to a healthy and mature self-sufficiency.

The Playboy is at once an extravagant comedy of situation and a dramatic bildungsroman in little. We witness the metamorphosis of a figure of farce into a dynamic character. A single moment in *All's Well That Ends Well,* after the exposure of Parolles, is similar to the ending of *The Playboy*.

> Yet I am thankful: if my heart were great
> 'Twould burst at this. Captain I'll be no more
> But I will eat and drink, and sleep as soft
> As captain shall: simply the thing I am
> Shall make me live.

The deflated boaster is suddenly human. Synge, however, goes beyond this affirmation of continued existence, and gives Christy a triumphant defiance of his persecutors. Where Shakespeare complicates the comic pattern by a moment of human reality, Synge turns it inside out, so that the scorned butt of laughter becomes the hero. Perhaps this is what Synge had in mind when he referred to the ambiguity of Shylock and Alceste in his letter defending *The Playboy*.

In a different way Synge manipulates the balance between comedy and realism in the figure of the Widow Quin. She originated in the earliest drafts of the play as the boldest of the hero-worshipping girls, appearing only in act 2. Changed from Sally Quin, when she was presumably Pegeen's contemporary, to the older and more experienced widow, she developed into one of Synge's favourite characters, and her part was expanded until for a time she looked like dominating the play. She seems at one point to be closer to Christy than Pegeen could ever be, with a feeling of loneliness very like Christy's:

> I'm above many's the day, odd times in great spirits, abroad in the sunshine, darning a stocking or stitching a shift, and odd times again looking out on the schooners, hookers, trawlers is sailing the sea, and I thinking on the gallant hairy fellows are drifting beyond, and myself long years living alone.

But Synge deliberately limited the widow's attractiveness and gave her only this one moment of seriousness. Once Christy decides definitely for Pegeen, she returns to her role as the cynical comic widow, bargaining for what she can get as she had done earlier with Shawn Keogh:

> CHRISTY (*with agitation*): . . . Will you swear to aid and save me for the love of Christ?
> WIDOW QUIN (*looks at him for a moment*): If I aid you, will you swear to give me a right of way I want, and a mountainy ram, and a load of dung at Michaelmas, the time you'll be master here?

She is completely reinstated as a figure of farce by the tag ending of the scene:

> Well if the worst comes in the end of all, it'll be great game to see there's none to pity him but a widow woman, the like of me has buried her children and destroyed her man.

Synge seems to have been in doubt whether or not to include these lines, and it was only in rehearsal that he decided to leave them in. They help to keep the widow well back from the edge of pathos.

The Widow Quin has a very functional part in the play; she is the stage manager of the piece, contriving action, supplying information, providing links between one scene and another. She is also something like the comic *raisonneur,* giving us a clear-sighted and realistic commentary on the action. Her view of Christy, for example, from the start is nearer the truth than that of the others: "it'd soften my heart to see you sitting so simple with your cup and cake, and you fitter to be saying your catechism than slaying your da." Her reactions are, on the whole, ordinary and normal, in so far as anyone is normal in *The Playboy*. Although she like the rest is impressed with the myth of the father-killer, she is "scandalised" at the depth of hatred she sees in Christy after Old Mahon has actually appeared. Her basic good nature is revealed again when all the others turn against him, and she tries to save him from the lynch-mob. And yet, although we can recognise the Widow's humanity, there seems to be something sordid and grotesque about her struggles to pin petticoats on the recalcitrant Christy. Her commonsensical decency and compassion is no longer relevant in the intensified emotional atmosphere of the concluding scenes, and, in fact, Synge allows her to vanish from the play without a final appearance. Like the Fool in *King Lear,* she is no longer needed. She can be no further help to Christy, for he has to lose all his allies in order to win through by himself. In the final series of confrontations between Christy and the crowd, Christy and Pegeen, Christy and his father, the shrewd and genial comic widow can have no part.

Comic convention throughout grows into a different sort of dramatic reality. Take, for example, the use of violence in the play. We can laugh at the story of Christy's deed in the opening scenes, by virtue of the comic immunity which dissociates violence from pain. "I just riz the loy and let fall the edge of it on the ridge of his skull, and he went down at my feet like an empty sack, and never let a grunt or groan from him at all." Our moral self-respect is protected by the comic guarantee of painlessness. It is a straightforward comic attitude which Synge encourages us to adopt to the story of the parricide, not "black" or "sick" comedy, where the laughter has an undercurrent of guilt. It is not even a satire on the specifically Irish sympathy for criminals. In spite of Synge's own professions and the instance of the Lynchehaun case which he said suggested the idea for the play, he does not focus directly on the rural Irish opposition to law. The comic convention established is basically independent of the local setting, and the unusual attitude to violence in Ireland is only of incidental relevance.

We can see this if we compare *The Playboy* with its "source" in *The Aran Islands*. Synge tells the story of the parricide whom the people sheltered and then comments on the islanders' attitude:

> If a man has killed his father, and is already sick and broken
> with remorse, they see no reason why he should be
> dragged away and killed by the law.
>
> Such a man, they say, will be quiet all the rest of his life,
> and if you suggest that punishment is needed as an exam-
> ple, they ask, "Would any one kill his father if he was able
> to help it?"

This is a profoundly moral response to a crime of violence: it implies
both an appreciation of the dreadfulness of the action, and the deep
remorse it must necessarily bring to the criminal. Synge also comments on the fact that the islanders dispatch a man judged guilty of a
crime, alone, to present himself at the jail in Galway where he is to
serve his sentence. This is not a lawless people, but one whose attitude to law is more sensitive than that of ordinary society.

Nowhere in *The Playboy* is the tone anything like that of the
simple unanswerable question, "Would any one kill his father if he
was able to help it?" Instead we have the interrogation of Christy
leading up to the splendid interchange:

> PEGEEN: Is it killed your father?
> CHRISTY: With the help of God I did surely, and that the
> Holy Immaculate Mother may intercede for his
> soul.

Of course Synge is putting to ironic effect the Irish custom of the
promiscuous invocation of the deity. But just as surely he is signal-
ling from the start that this is comedy, that we are not to consider
Christy's deed in its full moral implication. The inversion of values
indicated by Michael James's "great respect" for the parricide is part
of the comic convention. It is neither a direct nor a satiric portrayal of
the Irish peasants, in so far as they may be characterised as condoning
violence. Nobody outside a comedy, however anarchic, would say as
Pegeen does of a man who has killed his father—"That'd be a lad
with the sense of Solomon to have for a pot-boy." The very absurdity of the logic makes it impossible to take this seriously.

The Playboy starts with a comic hypothesis: a man who thinks
himself a parricide finds that he is not regarded with horror but with
respect, that he has come by means of his deed to a brave new world
of glory. What happens to the man as a result? Synge undoubtedly

took his cue for this hypothesis from the abnormal attitude to crime among the Irish country people, but it remains essentially a hypothesis, agreed between author and audience, as remote from ordinary reality as the absurd *malentendus* of farce. We can shamelessly enjoy Christy's full-scale account of the murder in act 2:

> CHRISTY: . . . Then I turned around with my back to the north, and I hit a blow on the ridge of his skull, laid him stretched out, and he split to the knob of his gullet. (*He raises the chicken bone to his Adam's apple.*)

At this climactic moment, any tendency we might have to consider the implications of splitting a man's head open is subverted by the gesture with the chicken bone. Long before Old Mahon appears on stage, we have realised that there is something unreal about Christy's deed, or at least attention has been comically arrested, so that we do not fully examine the reality of the murder.

Yet there is more than mock violence in *The Playboy*. Incidental remarks disturb the audience's attitude of comic anaesthesia. "Where now will you meet the like of Daneen Sullivan knocked the eye from a peeler, or Marcus Quin, God rest him, got six months for maiming ewes," says Pegeen complaining of the degeneracy of the times. Or again from Pegeen:

> You never hanged him, the way Jimmy Farrell hanged his dog from the licence and had it screeching and wriggling three hours at the butt of a string, and himself swearing it was a dead dog, and the peelers swearing it had life?

The same image is picked up when she frightens Christy with hanging in act 2: "it'd make the green stones cry itself to think of you swaying and swiggling at the butt of a rope." These lines are comic but it is a sardonic humour, for the description is rather too vivid for comfortable laughter. Where the fantastic absurdity of the playboy/parricide ensures a comic reaction, the hanging of the dog and the savagery of the "patriots" is closer to truth, less simply funny. Even more upsetting, because quite casual, is Widow Quin's warning to Old Mahon on the dangers of madness: "them lads caught a maniac one time and pelted the poor creature till he ran out raving and foaming and was drowned in the sea." We are given a horrifying glimpse of a community where madness is still laughable and cruelty commonplace.

Our comic attitude is unsettled by such passages, but it is only in the final act that violence suddenly becomes immediate and real. With the reappearance of Old Mahon and the exposure of Christy the emotional level of the play rises. Christy's humiliation is initially comic, but as Pegeen and the crowd turn on him, their cruelty becomes apparent. The climax comes as the taunted victim "swings round with a sudden rapid movement and picks up a loy." This loy has been used several times in the earlier scenes, when it needed only one look at it to start Christy off: "It was with a loy the like of that I killed my father." The comic prop now becomes a real instrument of violence, and the effect of Christy's movement on the audience is that of complete bewilderment. With the scene of the burning of Christy's leg, we are a long way from the comic security with which we received the news of his deed. Synge leads us across the "great gap between a gallous story and a dirty deed," from mock murder to real violence.

There is some evidence to suggest that it was this shattering of comic convention which provoked the reaction of the first-night audience. "The first act went well," according to Maire Nic Shiublaigh, "there was laughter at the right places and the correct degree of solemnity was maintained when it was demanded." The audience evidently accepted the fantastic plot—in this act as much as anywhere Irish men and women are shown hero-worshipping a parricide—and Lady Gregory was able to send a telegram to Yeats after the first act, announcing the play's success. But, Maire Nic Shiublaigh continues, "during the second act I began to feel a tenseness in the air around me." Padraic Colum, who was also present, thought that the audience started "growing hostile to the play from the point where Christy's father enters. That scene was too representational. There stood a man with horribly-bloodied bandage upon his head, making a figure that took the whole thing out of the atmosphere of high comedy." The line which actually started the row is well known (though it was apparently slightly altered on the night):

> What'd I care if you brought me a drift of chosen females, standing in their shifts itself maybe, from this place to the Eastern world.

It has been generally assumed that the puritanical Dubliners objected instantly to this vision of a nationwide harem, but it is worth noticing where the line comes in the play. Christy has just returned to the stage, apparently having murdered his father. It may well be that, after a few moments of stunned amazement, the audience reacted against this display of violence, and that it was all but accidental that the delayed response came at the word "shifts."

When the Abbey revived the play after Synge's death, they took care to avoid similar reactions:

> Originally that excellent actor W. G. Fay was in the part of the Playboy. He made the role a little sardonic, and this . . . took from the extravagance of the comedy. Afterwards the Playboy's father was made a less bloody object, and the part of the Playboy in the hands of another actor was given more charm and gaiety, and there was no trouble with the audience.

(A photograph of Fred O'Donovan as the playboy in 1910 makes clear the sort of conventional juvenile lead the part became.) In later productions *The Playboy* was played fast as a comedy, whereas "when it was given for the first time it was played seriously, almost sombrely." These remain the basic alternatives for directing the play. Both extravagant comedy and a more realistic form of drama are there and the central effect of the play depends upon the relation between the two.

The dramatic substance of *The Playboy* is so diverse that we cannot afford to abstract a theme and say—this is what the play is about. As soon as we formulate some such theme, the relation between fantasy and reality, the nature of role-playing, the growth of personality, it distorts the play's vision. The various levels of meaning which stand in relation like the terms of a fraction are then divided into a false decimal finality. The play is puzzling, and a common reaction to seeing or reading it for the first time is complete bewilderment. This bewilderment, however, is perfectly appropriate. In *The Playboy,* as in the other comedies, Synge is deliberately exploiting a pattern of unstable and fluctuating convention, so that uncertainty and confusion is built into his dramatic strategy. There are no shortcuts to the play's meaning. The success of *The Playboy* is that the precisely achieved structure holds together the different modes of action in a complex and resonant whole.

The Playboy as Antidrama

Bruce M. Bigley

Let me begin with a few observations on John Millington Synge's *The Playboy of the Western World* and its critical acceptance. It seems safe to assert that *The Playboy* is Synge's best play; although some prefer *Riders to the Sea,* they will agree that *The Playboy* is more characteristic and that it is the best full-length play. *The Playboy* is also one of the classics of modern British theater, probably the most anthologized modern full-length play written in English. More arguably, it is the finest play written in English in a couple of centuries. Hence we may say that it is highly regarded, it has worn well, it is worth study and rereading, and it has as unanimous a critical acclaim as one is likely to find in a twentieth-century author.

Yet there is little agreement on how to read the play or react to its title character. Is he a hero, a buffoon, a fraud, a Christ figure, a mock Christ, a Promethean figure, a demonic figure, an Oedipal figure, the last hero of the decadent West? Is he even the protagonist? And how are we to react to the peculiar ethics of the play: is parricide so good a thing as it seems to be? There is as little agreement critically about the genre of the play. Is it comedy, as Synge subtitles it; an extravaganza, as he called it in an unguarded moment; a comedy with an anticlimactic ending; tragicomedy; a comedy with a tragic ending (comitragedy?)? Northrop Frye avoids classifying it in the *Anatomy,* although he does remark elsewhere that Christy is a mutation of the *miles gloriosus;* but his disciples Foulke and Smith in *The Anatomy of*

From *Modern Drama* 20, no. 2 (June 1977). © 1977 by the University of Toronto, Graduate Centre for the Study of Drama.

Literature touch all of Frye's *mythoi* by describing it in the following manner: "a romantic hero has been built out of a tragic idea and immersed in a society that turns out to be ironic, yet this complex vision of human motives still ends in an exuberant celebration of the possibilities of life—elsewhere."

So on the level of character, of ethics, of genre, the play refuses to fit our categories; it constantly breaks down the barriers we have erected and then believed real. Probably for this reason our initial reaction to the play is, more often than delight, a puzzlement, if not anger. The play was disliked not only by the Irish nationalists who led the riots at its premiere, but also by such sympathetic viewers as George Moore and Lady Gregory. Moore objected to the ending as uncomic, although he later grew to see that it was right; and Lady Gregory became one of the play's champions on the first American tour. She could write in 1913 on *The Playboy*'s reception in America, "But works of imagination such as those of Synge could not be suppressed even if burned in the market place." Both recognized that the play would not fit into the comic scheme it invites us to impose, and eventually both seemed to understand that this quality is not a flaw, but the genius of the play. *The Playboy of the Western World* is actually less a mixture of comic and tragic elements than a denial of either convention, a kind of anticomedy and an antitragedy, indeed a kind of antidrama. The tonal shift toward the serious and brutal after the reentrance of Old Mahon in act 3 is only the final wrench to a play that keeps us uncomfortable from beginning to end. It is not a play written in ignorance of generic or ethical conventions. It depends for its effect on its rejection of convention. It is thus related to the tradition of theatricalist drama, to *The Rehearsal, The Green Cockatoo, Six Characters in Search of an Author,* and *Marat/Sade.* But it does not, like these plays, violate the illusion of the stage, although it does lead us to deny the naturalistic premise that we are determined by our environment, our stage setting. More importantly, it violates the generic conventions, the expectations it fosters in the audience, just as *Troilus and Cressida* repeatedly builds up and denies heroic expectations, or as *Bonnie and Clyde* encourages us to see crime as a joy ride and then shocks us with the inevitable blood. Synge carefully and skillfully manipulates our response to the material of the play in at least two ways: through our responses to generic convention he forces us into uncomfortable moral positions; and through our conventional moral responses he keeps us from settling into comfortable aesthetic attitudes.

For an example, let us look at Christy's first entrance. Christy Mahon enters into this village which is imaginatively starved by harsh, uncompromising poverty. The village is represented so far by Pegeen Mike, longing after Daneen Sullivan and Marcus Quin, two violent storytellers; by Shawn Keogh, with his borrowed vision of a theocracy in which the meek like himself will inherit their promised due; and by Michael James and his companions, who seek solace in drink. When Christy, his feelings hurt by Pegeen's accusation of innocence, and threatened by a beating, announces his crime—parricide—Pegeen Mike leads the others in offering admiration and awe. He becomes for each of them, except for Shawn, of course, the answer to a wish. Michael James and his companions see in him the solution to the immediate problem, finding a protector for Pegeen Mike for the night. Beyond this immediate goal he would provide the shebeen with protection from the peelers, since (according to their logic) the police are afraid of Christy. For Pegeen herself, he seems the embodiment of the rebel and the poet: he has struck his blow against authority, and he demonstrates, once drawn out, a way with language that will come to surpass them all. He is eligible to boot.

It is only Shawn who has his doubts about Christy, doubts that audiences and critics have shared since the appearance of the play. While Pegeen and the others feel awe, we feel with Shawn a certain horror for Christy's crime. But we are loath to associate our position with that of the village coward. The credibility of the villagers' acceptance of parricide as an admirable act, an acceptance we are forced uneasily to entertain, has been the main critical crux of the play. Synge recorded in *The Aran Islands* a similar instance, but the islanders only harbored a fugitive parricide rather than lionizing him. We naturally feel uneasy about the wholehearted acceptance of parricide as hero that the play seems to ask of us. With this uneasiness begins a carefully controlled counterpoint between the reactions of the villagers, Christy's audience on the stage, and the response of an audience in the theater. The audience on the stage reverse their earlier glorification when the act of parricide is reperformed in their presence; and they thereby lose their right to possess the Playboy of the Western World. The audience in the theater are spared the sight of an actual enactment of parricide, successful or not, and we can thus count ourselves on the winning side of Christy rather than on the losing side of Pegeen Mike. But we recognize quite surely at the end of the play that we probably belong with the lamenting Pegeen if not with the blind Shawn Keogh. So the dilemma of the audience in the first act persists throughout, although we are allowed some respite in the second act when we learn of the failure of the parricide. Our sympathies are in conflict and our reactions are ambivalent.

Christy's transformation and transcendence of the limits of reality in the Western World are based on his acceptance as actual of what the others were willing to accept as tall tale: an act in the imagination, if real, then distanced by time and space, without actual involvement for them, a gallous tale. When the act is reperformed in their presence, when they are called upon to reaffirm their complicity in a deed become real (apparently), they flee back to the world of the shebeen, bow to the authority of the English law, and rejoin Shawn's patriarchal society. The audience in the theater, since their sympathies have been separated from the beginning from Christy's audience on the stage, are left with the implicit responsibility to choose between Christy Mahon (and the uncomfortable implications of that choice, which range from parricide in act 1 to a rejection of "reality" in act 3) and Shawn Keogh (and the stifling implications of that choice, which always means bondage to "reality" or naturalism). The act of the imagination which frees Christy from the tyranny of the actual is revolutionary; and although the political currents in this play are less clearly relevant to the Irish Question than some have assumed, this revolution has social and political as well as psychological and epistemological implications.

"There's a great gap between a gallous story and a dirty deed," Pegeen Mike declares in one of the pivotal scenes of the last act, and most critics have seized upon this speech as somehow crystallizing the theme of Synge's problem play. Yet if we stop to measure it against the resolution of the plot, we must conclude, at the least, that for a character such as Christy Mahon has become by the end of the play, it is the story that determines reality: both the reality of character and the dominion of character over phenomenal reality. He learns, just as Synge's favorite poet learns in the course of *The Prelude*, "to what point, and how, / The mind is lord and master—outward sense / The obedient servant of her will." Just as the "spots of time" teach and continually remind Wordsworth that the imagination rightfully has dominion over phenomenal nature, so in another way Christy is taught to bridge the gap between the gallous story he tells and his own reality. But for Christy the experience means he must leave the social milieu which failed to learn this lesson even as it taught him. That a gallous story, a mere fiction, might be more important than what we so often think of as reality, the world of legal and economic obligations, is as disturbing a notion for us as it is for the inhabitants of the Western World in the play, and I would suggest that it is this element that is responsible for the peculiar reactions the play often elicits, not only the famous riots attending its première at the Abbey Theatre in 1907 and its first American tour in 1911, but also the discomfort we still feel today. Audiences are uncomfortable with the ambivalence of *The Playboy,* and they have too often preferred to reject the play rather than to consider the questions it raises. It is surely relevant that the riots on the premiere night occurred not in act 2 at the first appearance of the offending word *shifts,* but directly after the second parricide when the implication of the audience in the dilemma the play presents is most complex.

It is, of course, no accident that the deed that frees Christy from his dependence and allows him to grow into independent maturity is parricide. Whether we read Freud or Frazier or Blake, the resonance of that act is clear. But whatever we think of the symbolic nature of the act, what is important in the play is that it is a real act to Christy insofar as he twice strikes the blow and is prepared, the second time, and, if need be, a third time, to accept the consequences, both positive and negative. It is not, I think, the theme of parricide that disturbs us, but rather that the play teaches us that the reality we live in is not necessarily so well-founded as we believed. By accepting the implications of his dirty deed—even after he knows the deed itself to be false—Christy frees himself from what we usually call reality, a subjection to parental domination and its extensions in Church, state, and society. That domination of a materialistic vision forces Pegeen into a marriage with Shawn, even though he is a nonentity, because of his comparative wealth. This dependence on the materialistic has brutalized the imaginations of these villagers until, in reaction, their denied craving for something other leads them to drink, to slavish religiosity, or to the fascination with violence that imbues all their anecdotes to make a hero of a Marcus Quin, who maims ewes, not to mention Christy, the parricide. For the inhabitants of the Western World it is a confusion between the reality and the fiction that makes them goad Christy into the second murder and then assert the great gap between the story and the deed. For them the story of the murder was a tale separated from them by time, distance, and a narrator. The difference between Christy the epic hero and his creator, Christy the epic bard, is not understood, since for them whatever occurs outside the narrow world represented on the stage by the shebeen is unreal.

This distinction between Christy as hero and Christy as narrator is clear if we compare an early scenario with the play as it developed. Draft "E" of act 1 ends after Christy leaves in disgrace with his father in the following dialogue:

> BALLAD MAN (*singing as he comes in*):
> Young Christopher the daddy man came walking
> from Tralee
> And his father's bloody ghost the while did keep
> him company. . . .
> SHAWN (*jostling him*): Hold your jaw there his father's
> not murdered at all.
> BALLAD MAN: Oh, God help me and I after spending the
> half of me day making of his deed.
> SHAWN: He's not murdered I'm saying and we want
> none of your lies.
> BALLAD MAN: But it's a lovely song. . . .
> PEGEEN: What do we want with lies.
> BALLAD MAN: Well I'll sing it other roads where he's not
> known at all. It's a lovely song surely.
> SHAWN: Come on now to the green. (*Pipes are heard behind.*)
> There's the piper and we'll have great dancing till the
> fall of night.

Here the narrator-ballad singer transforms the deeds of Christy into a poem which has a raison d'être apart from its truth. He is only a step from the narrators of epic theater, the Stage Manager of *Our Town,* the narrator in *The Caucasian Chalk Circle,* or Tom in *The Glass Menagerie.* And he is closely related to the rumor mongers in Lady Gregory's *Hyacinth Halvey* and *Spreading the News.* But Synge goes on to identify Christy the protagonist with the narrator so that Christy the protagonist becomes an invention of Christy the narrator. The real action of the play is narration; and Christy learns that the craft of narration is independent of the category truth. To be sure he needs the encouragement of an audience. And his audience on the stage are made up of inveterate storytellers, so in act 1 they give Christy object lessons about the transformation of a dirty deed into a gallous story. But they never learn the relationship between truth and fiction.

Christy is able to learn because for him the first murder was real, until his father appears: the story has always had a basis in fact, even though it becomes more heroic with each retelling. He is ethically implicated, and he is willing to accept not only the reward, but the punishment. The shifting responses of the villagers to his story allow him to learn that the gap between a dirty deed and a gallous story is not so wide as to be unbridged. He proceeds to make a gallous story out of his hanging rather than collapse into a whimpering mass resigned to his fate (his reaction to act 2 to a lesser threat and now Shawn's reaction to Christy's bite):

> CHRISTY: If I can wring a neck among you, I'll have a royal judgment looking on the trembling jury in the courts of law. And won't there be crying out in Mayo the day I'm stretched upon the rope with ladies in their silks and satins snivelling in their lacy kerchiefs, and they rhyming songs and ballads on the terror of my fate? (*He squirms round on the floor and bites Shawn's leg.*)
>
> SHAWN (*shrieking*): My leg's bit on me! He's the like of a mad dog, I'm thinking, the way that I will surely die.
>
> CHRISTY (*delighted with himself*): You will then, the way you can shake out hell's flags of welcome for my coming in two weeks or three, for I'm thinking Satan hasn't many have killed their da in Kerry, and in Mayo too.

It is crucial that this affirmation occurs before Old Mahon reenters; Christy's growth is complete before we know that Old Mahon survives and therefore in no way dependent on Old Mahon's second survival, although presumably his own survival is, as is the ambivalent tonality of the play. Without Mahon's survival, the play would veer off into ironic tragedy, like *Bonnie and Clyde*.

In other words, Christy has learned that what we usually regard as literal reality is in fact unliteral, unliterary, or the raw material of an imaginative reshaping of it into a fiction. He teaches us to believe our ears, not our eyes, since our eyes tell us that Christy and the set remain the same through three acts, while our ears tell us that Christy has grown up and that the set changes for him as his vision of himself and reality expands. In act 1 the shebeen is a refuge from the police, but also a piece of real estate distinctly less desirable than his father's Kerry farm. In act 2, as he counts the wealth represented by jugs and glasses, it has become a place of comfort, potentially a dowry to be acquired. But by the love duet of act 3, it has become too confining a locale for Christy, so he offers Pegeen a "poacher's kind of love" in a natural setting. By his final exit he has learned that neither the shebeen nor Pegeen is worth having.

Significantly in the starkly naturalistic setting, the shebeen, almost nothing happens except narration, as if the poverty we see oppresses all other action. All the "real" events take place outside, in an unconfined setting, both of the murders and the games. Moreover the reference of the speeches, except for Christy's inventory in act 2, is always beyond the shebeen. Only the final skirmish takes place within the set, and it is at this point, when the action moves inside, that the reality becomes too much for the villagers and sometimes for the audience in the theater. Hence, they respond in the brutally defensive way of Michael James: "It is the will of God that all should guard their little cabins from the treachery of law and what would my daughter be doing if I was ruined or was hanged itself?" True reality in this play exists only beyond the back wall of the stage, and we can perceive it only indirectly, through the storytellers, the fabulists, mainly Christy, but also the others. In the race scene we perceive it in a sort of instant replay as told by Old Mahon, Widow Quin, Jimmy, and Philly. The villagers' imaginations are constantly expanding beyond the back wall to the bishops and the courts of Rome, to the polygamist Luthers of the preaching north, to the man who bit the yellow lady's nostril on the northern shore, to the parricide in Kerry. When that reality loses its comfortable distance and invades the shebeen, they retreat to the protection of Father Reilly, the English Courts, and the bottle. The audience in the theater, on the other hand, do not, because they have been not only educated along with Christy in the poetic process, but also spared an immediate vision of the reality out there. But Christy has been out there—although he does not realize it until he stumbles into the shebeen and learns with the help of these naturalistic victims that he need not simply react to reality, that he can shape it to suit his desires. He can shape an otherwise dirty deed into a gallous story.

Christy's ability to transform reality through the story, this apparent lack of connection with the facts, may incline us to dismiss the play and Synge as escapist. But we must recognize a theme which weighs against this dismissal. Christy's reality beyond the stage wall, like Deirdre's in Synge's last play, is not totally arbitrary like the reality of Algernon in *The Importance of Being Earnest*. It is a natural order. One can grasp this point by comparing Christy to Hjalmar Ekdal in Ibsen's *Wild Duck*, a character who also uses words to reduce an unhappy "reality" to a kind of story with himself as hero (although Hjalmar's preferred genre is melodrama, not epic). But Hjalmar's imaginative world, his green world as it were, centers in a garret filled with some old Christmas trees, chickens, rabbits, and a wild duck quickly becoming domestic. Christy's green world is nature and the inspiration of his language is natural. It is a world which includes, besides the natural pleasures, winter and hunger and cold and aging and death. Most of all it includes loneliness. These aspects are implicit in the *Playboy,* especially in Christy's natural imagery, but they are explicit in *Deirdre of the Sorrows.* In the latter, Deirdre voluntarily ends a "playgirl" existence and seeks certain death; she chooses to avoid the waning of love and beauty which is inescapable, though the inhabitants of Emain Macha try to deny that natural process. The theme is also clear in Synge's first play, *In the Shadow of the Glen,* where the tramp invites Nora to leave her dull, jealous husband to join him in a vagrant existence that includes both pleasures and pains:

> We'll be going now, I'm telling you, and the time you'll be feeling the cold and the frost, and the great rain, and the sun again, and the south wind blowing in the glens, you'll not be sitting . . . in this place, making yourself old with looking on each day and it passing you by. You'll be saying one time, "It's a grand evening by the grace of God," and another time. "It's a wild night, God help us, but it'll pass surely."

On the other hand it is the world we usually call realistic, represented by Byrne's cottage, Emain Macha, and O'Flaherty's shebeen, that tries to deny the reality of time and death and pain. A whole series of characters in Synge from Dan Burke in *The Shadow* through Widow Casey in the *Playboy* and Conchubar in *Deirdre* try to purchase the youth they have wasted in "realistic" matters through grotesquely younger spouses: Nora, Christy, and Deirdre. Material wealth in Synge is always used as an attempt to buy time, and Christy is most disappointing at the beginning of act 2, where he seems to believe the shebeen with its "power of glasses" is enough to make him happy. Parricide, real or symbolic, becomes necessary when an older generation tries through power or wealth to deny time by subjugating the younger generation whose time has come. It is the villagers in the Western World, materially so poor, who are afraid to accept the reality of time and the passing of power from one generation to the next. Old Mahon accepts with a broad smile and a "Glory be to God!"

Many of the difficulties the play presents can be resolved by seeing it, not as a comedy, which we are invited to do, but as a *Bildungsdrama* in which Christy grows from a timid lad, dominated by his father, something like Shawn Keogh, to a confident, self-reliant artist, like his father, master of his circumstances, chiefly through his mastery of language. He flees his home to wander in the world and finds the needed impetus for his growth in the admiration of the villagers and of Pegeen Mike for him and for his "gallous story." But by the last scene he has liberated himself from dependence on them just as surely as he had from dependence on the truth of his story and earlier from dependence on his father. He will "go romancing through a romping lifetime from this hour to the dawning of the judgement day"; or, to qualify his hyperbole, until he becomes subject to the natural limitations of aging, just as his father has become subject to one of those hazards, a son who asserts his independence. This limited qualification of Christy's assertion is implicit in his language, because he rejects allegiance never to the natural reality of time and mutability, but only to the social realities of the world as represented by the shebeen and its grudging submission to Father Reilly and the English law.

This pattern is one we are used to in fiction, especially in the tradition of the bildungsroman, in which typically a hero moves from a position of social and familial conformity to the freedom of a conscious independence from that conformity. One might mention the roughly contemporaneous Stephen Dedalus or Hans Castorp. But this pattern of plot is much less common in drama, where there is a stronger pressure toward social conformity which is inherent in the very mode of theater and the mechanics of its performance. Christy changes more radically than almost any character in drama—the only similar transformation I can think of is Sigismund in Hofmannsthal's

Der Turm, although Wagner's Siegfried and Giraudoux's Electre also grow to maturity before our eyes. The problem of making Christy's rapid transformation believable explains some of the measures Synge had to take, most significantly Christy's passivity as protagonist.

Our most traditional dramatic patterns also turn on the conflict of an individual with society, but society usually triumphs. Even where there is a conflict between two individuals, it is the individual most attuned to social values who triumphs. If this characterization of drama is fair, then clearly the *Playboy* is unusual as traditional drama. It would more clearly fit the pattern if the society of the village and Pegeen had been able to forgive Christy his unwitting lie after either of Old Mahon's resurrections, so that Christy's extravagances might have been integrated into the society as comic tall tales; or alternatively, if Christy had left as either a fugitive, a prisoner of the police, or just an exile, but without our approval and Pegeen's lament. But it is clear from Synge's revisions that he consistently moves away from the traditional comic situation toward more and more ambiguous patterns. The play seems to fit into the very typical ironic comic pattern of *Tartuffe* or *Volpone,* in which the imposter is finally unmasked and rejected as society closes its ranks, but for the fact that *The Playboy of the Western World* leaves the audience, like Pegeen, feeling trapped in the ranks of a restrictive society and longing for the freedom of the imposter. The implications of this "comedy" are antisocial, hence uncomic and undramatic in a fundamental way. If we consider that the only action central to the play is narration and that the community created by the play is a community only in its sharing of an aesthetic response to Christy's story, not in any sharing of an interpretation of the facts, the ethics, or even the genre of the play, we can conclude that *The Playboy of the Western World* is truly antidrama, a form which undercuts its own conventions and refuses to resolve the problems it raises.

The Gallous Story and the Dirty Deed: The Two *Playboys*

Edward Hirsch

The Playboy of the Western World is the most controversial play in Irish history. When *The Playboy* was first produced in January 1907, it sparked a turbulent week of demonstrations and riots. Even such a devotee of the Dublin theater as Joseph Holloway labeled the play "Blackguardism!" and Synge "The evil genius of the Abbey." Yet Synge's "able lieutenant" and most incisive early commentator, W. B. Yeats, immediately responded to the "mischievous extravagance" and verbal brilliance of the play, and he considered the failure of the audience to understand it the one serious failure of the Irish dramatic movement. During the length of its first production the play spawned a diversity of opinions which in effect break down into two violently opposed camps, represented by Yeats on one side and the opening-night Abbey audience on the other. The Yeatsian, or modernist, reading of Synge emphasized how much of the mind of Ireland the play contained, while praising its imaginative extravagance and exuberance, its satiric force, and, perhaps most crucially, its rich linguistic plenitude. The initial audience, responding to what it understood as the representational mode of *The Playboy,* dismissed the portrayal of Irish life as false naturalism, and objected to the plot and the language of the play on social and political grounds. The audiences who rioted in New York and Philadelphia in 1911–12

From *Modern Drama* 26, no. 1 (March 1983). © 1983 by the University of Toronto, Graduate Centre for the Study of Drama.

when the Irish actors took the play on tour were heirs to the representational "reading" of Synge.

Most of Synge's subsequent literary commentators have followed the Yeatsian tradition of reading. Thus, most literary critics have accepted that *The Playboy* exists "in the realms of fantasy or phantasmagoria" (Seán Ó Tuama) and that the play's actions "make no pretence to realism" (Alan J. Bliss). Clearly, Synge's first reviewers in both the nationalist *and* the unionist presses thought otherwise. The *Sinn Féin* writer categorically announced that "the author of the play presents it as true to Irish life" ("The Abbey Theatre," 2 February 1907); similarly the *Irish Times*'s reviewer suggested that "Mr. Synge set himself the task of introducing his audience to a realistic picture of peasant life in the far west of Ireland" ("Abbey Theatre," 28 January 1907). The modernist and representational ways of encountering *The Playboy* face each other in inevitable conflict. Indeed, sometimes the space between them seems as great as what Pegeen Mike identifies as the "great gap between a gallous story and a dirty deed."

One way to respond to this critical gap is simply by dismissing the reactions of the Dublin audience. This has been the fundamental strategy adopted by almost all critics. If anything, the controversy over *The Playboy* has usually been invoked to sustain the myth of Synge as an unwitting victim, an innocent genius howled down by cultural philistines. Alan Price puts forward the conventional opinion when he states that "the fierce assaults upon Synge during his lifetime . . . are not, in any sense, literary comment or criticism that merits consideration." It has been axiomatic for several generations of Synge critics to summarize the controversy by stating that the Dublin (and the later Irish-American) playgoers had narrow political and moral values but no literary or aesthetic values. Yet a playgoer without aesthetic values is a strange creature to contemplate, since no play can elicit response (and certainly not with the vehemence of the Abbey audience on opening night) without some aesthetic conventions for interpreting, understanding, and evaluating it. No doubt there were a vast number of people who objected to the moral, religious, and political content of the play without ever hearing it, or like the minor Abbey playwright William Boyle, without ever attending a performance. Yet the very frequency with which the issue of the play's realism was invoked by Synge's opponents should alert us to the literary dimensions of the first audience's responses. Those hostile responses were in part a reaction to the controversial realism of the play, a realism that is simultaneously asserted and denied as the action unfolds. The key question which has seldom been asked is still: to what extent does the play affirm its own typicality? Does it at all represent itself as representative? To the degree that it does posit its own realistic status, the audience's social, moral, and political responses may be viewed as the outgrowth of a problematic, but nonetheless real, literary experience.

The essentially urban, Catholic, middle-class spectators at the Abbey Theatre on opening night were encountering a play by an Anglo-Irish Protestant writer which seemed to establish its own representational intent, but which did not then provide what they considered a conventional or adequate representation of peasant life. In other words, the realistic mode of discourse established generic expectations in the audience which were then subverted as the plot developed. To understand the audience's volatile response to this subversion, it is necessary to remember how deeply the concept of the Irish peasantry was encoded with political meaning. It has often been said that Synge was "apolitical," a characterization undeniably true if one defines "political" by an interest in current affairs and partisan issues. But in the context of early twentieth-century Ireland, to dramatize the peasantry in any way was in itself a "political" act, endowed with ideological significance. Both to the playwright and to his audience, the Irish peasant was important not for his own sake but for what he signified as a concept and as a language. To speak about the "peasant" was to share a vocabulary; simultaneously, to undermine and attack one's idea of the peasant was to come uncomfortably close to attacking one's class concept of Ireland. It was not necessarily naive or paranoid for the Abbey audience to believe that *The Playboy*'s apparent representation of the Irish countryman as a "murderous savage" might have negative political consequences, since no dramatization of Irish peasant life could be wholly free of the looming shadow and presence of the English colonizer.

A single example illustrates how charged the issue of representing the peasant in art could be: the reader of most English newspapers in 1907 could still find striking caricatures of the Irish peasant, but as L. Perry Curtis, Jr., has documented, the ethnic stereotypes of the late Victorian and early modern era were far more dangerous than the equivalent caricatures of the mid-nineteenth century. Curtis writes: "The gradual but unmistakable transformation of Paddy, the stereotypical Irish Celt of the mid-nineteenth century, from a drunken and relatively harmless peasant into a dangerous ape-man or simianized agitator reflected a significant shift in the attitudes of some Victorians about the differences between not only Englishmen and Irishmen, but also between human beings and apes." This dehumanization of the Irish in English cartoons (and also on the stage) was fiercely challenged by the alternative tradition in Irish cartoons of portraying the peasant as a noble, honest, victimized farmer. These rival portraits of the Irish peasant were never far from any Irish audience's political consciousness.

It is not surprising, then, to find the Dublin audience reacting with overt hostility to Synge's attack on the nationalist belief in an idealized Catholic peasant, especially when he supplanted that image with his own representation of the violence and verbal extravagance at the center of Irish country life. That portrayal seemed especially offensive since it was presented in a nationalist theater that had been founded to counter the traditional stereotypes of the stage Irishman. In reading the character of Christy Mahon as another example of the colonial stereotype, the audience misread the degree to which he is a parody of the conventional figure. At the same time, the transformation of Christy from a mock into a real playboy is also a parody of the pious idealization of the Irish countryman created by the patriots. The play unquestionably challenges the prevailing platitudes about country life: in fact, Synge's characters were designed to contradict and undermine the normative concept of the peasantry. In an early draft of his essay "The People of the Glens," Synge commented on the current fashion in Dublin "to exalt the Irish peasant into a type of almost absolute virtue, frugal, self-sacrificing, valiant." Sounding the harsh Rabelaisian note was an aggressive attempt to deflate the audience's romantic pastoralism.

Of course, neither the Irish middle class's sentimentalization of the Gaelic peasant as a noble and virtuous patriot, nor the Syngeian version of that same peasant as a primitive or "natural" as opposed to a "cultural" being, has any basis in social or historical reality. Indeed, the whole concept of an unchanging Irish peasantry has been called into question by F. S. L. Lyons, who suggests that "the general effect of the economic changes in the second half of the nineteenth century was to substitute a rural bourgeoisie for a rural proletariat" in the Irish countryside. Martin J. Waters has in turn argued that few

aspects of Irish life were unaffected by the massive social and economic transformations in nineteenth-century Irish life: "The notion,
then, of an 'Irish peasantry' with a peculiar ethos somehow remain-
ing outside the dynamics of Irish history . . . is untenable." That the
peasants may no longer have existed by the time of the *Playboy* riots
should suggest that it is not so much what real peasants were, but
what they represented, that mattered to playgoer and author alike.
And "peasants" could be used effectively to communicate in the theater precisely because they already existed as myths in both the social
and political *and* the literary and cultural consciousness.

The *Playboy*'s assault on the myth of a noble Irish peasant is
presented within a fictive frame, but the highly flammable political
implications of the play continually threatened to dissolve that frame.
In a perceptive letter to the *Freeman's Journal* ("Mr. Boyle and Mr.
Synge," 2 February 1907), the critic Stephen Gwynn noted the
potential effect of the play in the nonplay world without denying its
status as an aesthetic object:

> Artistically I have not a word to say against Mr. Synge, for
> the facts out of which his exaggeration springs exist
> unquestionably, and no good critic will take his play as a
> social document, a literal impeachment, of the Irish
> country people. But practically I recognize that if the play
> succeeded it would be held as justifying the view which
> represents Ireland as peopled by a murderous race of
> savages.

Conor Cruise O'Brien has also suggested that the early Abbey audiences were insecure in their own raw Anglicization and "tortured by
the thought of English ridicule"; consequently, they often felt betrayed by the treachery of Protestant writers like Yeats and Synge.
For the Dublin audiences, then, the Irish peasant could be exploited
as a source of pride and/or shame. What has seldom been recognized
is how explicitly *The Playboy* preyed on its spectators' feelings and
insecurities, defiantly setting out to betray and assault their urban,
Catholic, middle-class values. To reconstruct the nature of the original response to *The Playboy* is to document historically the way in
which a modernist text can affront the values and mores of a middle-
class audience. By marshaling information and carefully constructing
a situation in order to build up a response, and then by radically

undercutting and denying that response, *The Playboy* attacked its first audience, thus employing a characteristic modernist tactic, the method and politics of assault.

The Playboy has created two diametrically opposed strategies for its own interpretation. A characteristic of each of these strategies is to deny and attack the other. Consequently, by responding to the representational *Playboy,* the audience either ignored the play's vital mode of satirical farce, or else translated that mode into the inadequate channel of realism, thus reacting to the play as a social/political message. This reaction in turn led to vituperative counterattacks, the tone and temper of which can be gauged by this statement from "The People and the Parricide," in *Freeman's Journal* (29 January 1907): "The stage Irishman is a gentleman in comparison with the vile wretch whom Mr. Synge presented to an astonished Irish audience as the most popular type of the Irish peasant." In contrast, the modernist interpretation of *The Playboy* denies the play's social/political implications by denying its representational claims and privileging its extravagance and theatricality. So in his numerous comments about the play, Yeats continually emphasized that all art is exaggeration, an opinion sanctioned by Synge in several statements to the press. Both Yeats and Synge were subsequently contemptuous of the audience's uncultivated middle-class reactions. The tone and temper of their contempt can be judged by Yeats's famous poem "On Those That Hated 'The Playboy of the Western World,' 1907":

> Once, when midnight smote the air,
> Eunuchs ran through Hell and met
> On every crowded street to stare
> Upon great Juan riding by:
> Even like these to rail and sweat
> Staring upon his sinewy thigh.

So great is the discrepancy between these two types of responses that it is almost as if they were referring to different events or texts. And in some ways they were. The gap between the Yeatsian response to *The Playboy* as a theatrical exaggeration and the response to it as a referential work suggests not only different ideas about the play (and about literature itself), but also different interpreters responding to alternative codes within *The Playboy*. This effect is not accidental. Synge has designed a language that conveys two opposing codes linked to two different value systems; these value systems have in turn been manifested by the contradictory demands of the social and literary audiences. In setting the middle-class code against the aesthetic or theatrical code, *The Playboy* sets the urban, nationalist, and middle-class audience against the literati. Despite the protestations of critics that the original Dublin audience's response was not literary, the evidence suggests that the juxtaposition and mix of codes are inherent features of the text itself.

Conceiving *The Playboy* as a representational drama of Irish peasant life has been in disfavor for over half a century, partially because such an interpretation of the play means taking the side of the original audience against the artist. In essence, the audience's response to the opening-night performance was a referendum on the play's realism. It is in the nature of literary realism to deny its own aesthetic nature, to pose as a truthful account of social life. But realism is nonmimetic. Roland Barthes has argued that it is the essential middle-class form precisely because it functions by turning bourgeois culture into nature ("Life"), thus fulfilling the requirements of bourgeois ideology. This process has nothing to do with reportage, but rather concerns mobilizing the stereotypes of social discourse for the purpose of making them appear universal. Middle-class audiences go to the theater to see realistic plays not because they want real life on the stage (this is exactly what they do not want), but because they want their own ideology inscribed in art. At center stage in the realistic text is always the "character": an identification circuit with the audience is established through "character." The more an audience recognizes itself in the "character," the more marketable and popular a form of literature the aesthetic object becomes. The reverse is also true: when the characters in a play do not fulfill the norms of a middle-class audience, the less familiar and recognizable they seem. When those characters actively subvert and contradict the norms, when they introduce recognizable social types only to dismantle them, the audience also feels subverted and undermined. This is what happened at the first performance of *The Playboy*. By the third act, the subversion of characters was interpreted as a frontal attack on the audience's ideology. This reaction led in turn to the breakdown of the play's rhetorical conventions, the necessary cooperative relationship between the actors and the spectators.

It is precisely because the Dublin audience recognized *The Playboy*'s realistic markers (while missing or misreading the play's extravagance) that it reacted as it did, rejecting what it interpreted as the play's claims to being representative. Even before the play appeared, the *Freeman's Journal* (26 January 1907) carried a preliminary announcement, most likely supplied by the theater management with Synge's approval, which emphasized both Synge's knowledge of the Irish peasantry and the play's truthfulness. As such, this announcement anticipated some of the critiques later leveled by nationalists:

> *No one is better qualified than Mr. Synge to portray truthfully the Irish peasant* living away in Western Ireland. He has lived with them for months at a stretch, in the Arran [*sic*] Islands and Mayo. He has noted *their speech, their humours, their vices, and virtues.* He is one of the best Irish speakers in the country, and is thus brought into the closest contact with people. *"The Playboy" is founded on an incident that actually occurred.*

The explicit suggestion that there is *no one* in Ireland better *qualified* than Synge to portray *truthfully* the Irish peasant is part of the message of the play. Synge supplied a program note for the first production which also served as an advance public defense of the play:

> In writing "The Playboy of the Western World," as in my other plays, I have used very few words that I have not heard among the country people, or spoken in my own childhood before I could read the newspapers. . . . Nearly always when some friendly or angry critic tells me that such or such a phrase could not have been spoken by a peasant, he singles out some expression that I have heard, word for word, from some old woman or child, and the same is true also, to some extent, of the actions and incidents I work with. The central incident of the Playboy was suggested by an actual occurrence in the west.

In both apologias, Synge was arguing rhetorically for the play's credibility, implicitly placing his own vision of peasant life against the more conventional received opinion. Rather than forestalling criticism, this strategy helped to create it. The audience translated these realistic markers into generic terms with which it was familiar. Thus, instead of *The Playboy*, the audience was led to expect a typical Irish peasant comedy in the mode of social realism. The audience at the Abbey was making a time-bound aesthetic judgment in terms of its previous literary experience. The original reception of *The Playboy* may be explicable in literary terms by the fact that the play carefully established expectations in its audience of a realistic drama of western Ireland treated in conventional terms. When the play began to disturb and flout those conventional norms in a radically charged and meaningful way, the audience felt assaulted by the text. With this effect in mind, the critic no longer finds it possible to consider either the press release or the program note "innocently," or as descriptions without literary intent. Synge's claims to linguistic and ethnographic fidelity created expectations (the audience after all had its own pastoral vision of the western world) which were then exploded by the violent and unrealistic mode of *The Playboy*. At the same time, the harsh Rabelaisian note of the play kept the audience from dismissing it as a simple fictional extravaganza. Thus, a kind of double-bind situation was created.

Another fact reveals that the audience could not respond to the play simply as an extravagant comedy: *The Playboy* was charged not only with producing a false portrait of Irish life, but also with presenting a too literal portrait of that life. The most common complaint was against the coarseness of the dialogue. The play characterizes the Irish country people, but its verbal extravagance was directed to and could not but offend the proprieties of the Dublin audience. The writer in the *Irish Times* ("Abbey Theatre," 28 January 1907) objected to presenting actual peasant speeches in the theatrical context:

> While there is not a word or a turn of expression in the play that is not in common use amongst peasants, it is quite another matter to reproduce some of the expressions on a public stage. . . . People here will not publicly . . . submit to the reproduction of expressions which, to say the least, are offensive to good taste, however true they may be to actual life.

On the opening night the angry audience finally erupted over the so-called offensive word "shifts," though it should be evident that more than a single word was at issue. William Fay's substitution of "Mayo girls" in Christy's famous image of "a drift of chosen females, standing in their shifts itself maybe, from this place to the Eastern World" seemed to reinforce the play's aggressive claim to realism. Synge defended his usage by saying that the word "was an everyday word in the west of Ireland, which would not be taken offence at there" ("Abbey Theatre Scene," *Evening Telegraph*, 29 January 1907). But insofar as it is true, his citation of the fact that the word appeared without objection in Douglas Hyde's *Love-Songs of Connacht* (1893) helps to establish that the word was offensive not so much in itself as in the symbolic fictional context where it appeared. The frame was crucial. And the audience's vehement response ruptured that frame, in effect defictionalizing the drama. For the opening-night audience, *The Playboy* crossed the limits of theatrical convention and the dramaturgical frame could no longer dominate the social frame. This interpretation of the outbreak is consistent with Padraic Colum's testimony that the audience began to grow hostile from the moment in act 2 when Christy's father, old Mahon, enters the stage wearing a "horribly-bloodied bandage," because "That scene was too representational." The literal details of the scene began to challenge both the comic tone and the larger fictional frame. The standing evidence of Christy's failed parricide shocked his stage audience and prodded *The Playboy*'s real one. It is in this context that the final eruption must be understood.

It is not surprising, then, to find the complaint against *The Playboy*'s dialogue paralleled by a complaint against its dark thematic literalism. The reporter in the *Irish Times* ("Pat," "That Dreadful Play," 30 January 1907) argued that "The idle aim of a mere extravaganza does not justify the grimly realistic treatment of a distinctly unpleasant theme." When William Fay tried to quiet the audience during the second performance, a voice called out, "Such a thing as is represented could not occur in Ireland." Again the interpretive premise is clear: *The Playboy* was a drama claiming more than fictive status. This interpretation was reinforced again when Synge's preface was published with its celebrated story of how he had listened to servant girls through a chink in the floor of an old Wicklow house during the composition of *In the Shadow of the Glen*. By emphasizing his unobtrusive and empirical method of gaining access to speech in its "natural" habitat, Synge was simultaneously claiming special authority for the language of his plays and defending their authenticity. The preface, written after *The Playboy* but printed before it, was an attempt to guide or reframe and thus defend the literary event which the audience (or the reader) was about to experience.

It should now be fairly evident that Synge hedged on the issue of the play's mode, in essence authorizing contradictory and mutually exclusive interpretations. On the one hand, he hinted at the many-sided nature and multiple codes of *The Playboy* by suggesting in a public letter that " 'The Playboy of the Western World' is not a play with 'a purpose' " and that "There are, it may be hinted, several sides to 'The Playboy.' " On the other, he emphasized its ethnographic reality. In fact, whenever his knowledge of peasant life was questioned during the *Playboy* controversy, he responded by pointing out again the tale's original sources. By invoking the Aran incident on which the play is partially based, Synge was both positing the play's verifiability and affirming its strange naturalistic stratum. Ironically, in defending his work by establishing its empirical base, Synge appeared to be encouraging a too literal response to his work.

The Playboy begins by showing Pegeen dressed in *"the usual peasant dress,"* writing a letter at a table in a typical *"very rough and untidy"* country public house, the social center of the district. The overdetermined and detailed catalog of items which Pegeen lists to herself as she writes (extending from "Six yards of stuff for to make a yellow gown" to "A fine tooth comb," all "To be sent with three barrels of porter in Jimmy Farrell's creel cart on the evening of the coming Fair") helps to establish a firm naturalistic frame. The subsequent dialogue between Pegeen and her timid suitor, Shawn Keogh, also creates the expectation of a realistic peasant comedy. But what the audience would eventually interpret as the play's critical representations of the Irish country people is soon voiced in Pegeen's scornful response to Shawn's boast that "we're as good this place as another":

> PEGEEN (*with scorn*): As good, is it? Where now will you
> meet the like of Daneen Sullivan knocked the eye
> from a peeler, or Marcus Quin, God rest him, got
> six months for maiming ewes, and he a great war-
> rant to tell stories of holy Ireland till he'd have the
> old women shedding down tears about their feet.
> Where will you find the like of them, I'm saying?

It is still possible at this point in the play to evaluate Pegeen's fierce characterization of the country people within the tradition of local color (and also as a rhetorical counter to Shawn's timidity). But from the moment that Christy Mahon bashfully and miserably enters the scene and is slowly coaxed into telling his story, the play begins to subvert its realistic conventions.

The prose naturalism of the initial scene soon modulates into the implausibility of a plot in which a stranger's tale of parricide makes him a local hero, "the champion playboy of the Western World." Thereafter the inclusive naturalistic frame is continually being violated by the fantastic speeches and responses of the characters. To an audience working within the confines of the realistic mode of discourse, it would soon begin to seem that fantasy was being claimed as representation. The later objection to Christy as a stage Irishman was a reaction to perceiving a stereotype masquerading as the truthful character sketch of a typical figure. Similarly, the real audience found no one in Christy's play-audience with whom it could identify or sympathize. Between Pegeen's irresponsible father and her cousin's whimpering cowardice, the male characters are uniformly unappealing, either unwilling or unable to protect the bored females. And the females are wholly entranced by the playboy's story of his crime. When Christy announces that "I'm not calling to mind any person, gentle, simple, judge or jury, did the like of me," his audience draws round him with delighted surprise. At the beginning of act 2, when Christy admits to the village girls that he is the man who killed his father, they respond with gifts and a "thousand welcomes to you."

Christy's growth into a real playboy is primarily a result of the awed welcome of Pegeen and the other females in the play. It is no wonder, then, that he is forced to conclude in the closing lines of act 1: "I'm thinking this night wasn't I a foolish fellow not to kill my father in the years gone by." The psychosexual implications of Christy's apparently apt conclusion that killing his father earlier would have made him into a sexual hero earlier could only make a middle-class Catholic audience extremely uneasy. (That uneasiness was directly manifested when they broke up over the word "shifts.") Thus, the response by the local people to Christy's grim tale of parricide created an increasingly large gap between the fictive and the live audiences' sympathies. By being placed in a parallel relationship to the text, the real audience (the playgoer) was forced to watch its counterpart (the play-audience) creating an unacceptable hero. So much of the play is concerned with role-playing that one suspects this parallel was being ironically manipulated. Certainly this widening gap helps to explain why, as the plot unfolded and Christy gradually began to assume the features of the fictional protagonist he had accidentally created, the play was increasingly interpreted as an aggressive authorial act.

The alternative representation of *The Playboy* as a modernist comedy defines itself against the responses of the first audience. Whether explicitly (as in Yeats's case) or implicitly (as in the case of most critics), the strategy of reading the play as a modernist text is designed to undermine and attack the claims to *The Playboy*'s representational nature, in essence denying the middle-class code of the play. Yeats first established this tradition by claiming that the play's fantastic mode placed it not in a tradition of realism, but within the aristocratic literary tradition of Irish fantasy. He was thus both establishing an Irish lineage for the play, and countering the nationalist strategy of reducing *The Playboy* to a social document and therefore defining literary values by their political consequences. The key to the modernist *Playboy* is the play's exuberant language, its play of signifiers, which includes a compendium of other languages and styles: courtly Irish love poetry, Elizabethan rhetoric, French Symbolist verbiage. All of these linguistic styles point to the aesthetic nature of the play. By continually referring to and incorporating other languages as languages, *The Playboy* is also continually directing attention to itself, to its own vital and extravagant poetry.

In fact, the play insistently converts the characters' speeches into poetry and lets us know that it is doing so. These speeches thus become important as celebrations both of the Irish language and of the play which explores and re-creates that language. In particular, the characters often comment on Christy's verbal brilliance. For example, Christy tells his "gallous" story to Pegeen and the other villagers with such skill that she accuses him of telling it "in every cot and cabin where you've met a young girl on your way." His exclamatory denial brings forth this delighted compliment: "If you weren't destroyed travelling, you'd have as much talk and streeleen, I'm thinking, as Owen Roe O'Sullivan or the poets of the Dingle Bay." In act 2 Pegeen again responds to Christy's "infinite admiration" by asking: "Would you have me think a man never talked with the girls would have the words you've spoken to-day?" One event in particular suggests that the playboy and his language become stand-ins for the playwright and his: when Christy wins the races he is awarded a bagpipe, "A fiddle was played by a poet in the years gone by!", and a blackthorn stick "would lick the scholars out of Dublin town!"; these prizes all indicate the traditional consecration of an Irish bard. Indeed, Christy is sometimes astonished by the words and metaphors that issue from his own mouth: "I'm after hearing my voice this day saying words would raise the topknot on a poet in a merchant's town.'' By continually celebrating his own words, *The Playboy* turns language into the most important actor in the play.

The self-reflexive nature of *The Playboy*'s style, the first condition of its modernity, draws attention away from what the play represents and toward style itself as an aesthetic entity, an object in its own right. The verbal extravagance becomes a testament and a dramatization of the generative power of the Irish language that can create an endless number of metaphors and images, tales and myths as a source for the artist. The idea of a perfect generating language is reified by the critics who have continually demonstrated that the play creates a variety of different mythologies and antimythologies; thus Christy has been considered a mock Cuchulain, a mock Oedipus, a Christ figure, a mock Christ figure, a self-actualizing romantic poet, and a parody of a romantic poet. All of these readings privilege the modernist code of the play in contrast to that of the Irish middle-class audience who wanted language to celebrate Irish objects (and not itself) and Irish historical progress (and not literary history). For that audience, the Irish peasant was more than a source for literary mythology or an opportunity for linguistic play.

Critics have been implicated in the modernist strategy of *The Playboy* by ignoring or denying that the Irish peasant was encoded with political meaning. But to suppress that fact is to suppress a crucial feature of the play itself. In effect, the audience was being asked to give up the politically encoded figure of the peasant by laughing at it and to submit to Synge's aesthetic rewriting of the figure in literary language. But for the urban, Catholic, middle-class audience, the Irish countryman functioned as an autochthonous myth, the source of all authentic Irish life. That peasant was a symbol of colonial dissent; and being physically rooted in Irish soil, he also established irrefutable property rights and economic claims to Ireland against the English colonizer. This economic idea of the peasant was different from the idea promulgated by the Anglo-Irish Protestant writers of the literary revival who spiritualized the peasant by dematerializing him, turning him into ''natural'' and antieconomic man. The romanticization of the peasant imagination as a visionary enbodiment of the ancient Celtic imagination could then be used as a foil against the materialism of the current age, and the peasant could be held up as a pastoral ideal opposed to the Dublin middle classes.

Consequently, the audience was being asked to submit to a

reformulation of peasant life which directly attacked its own idea of that life. To refuse submission was, however, to forgo the aesthetic pleasures of the play and, consequently, as a history of readers has confirmed, to label oneself a cultural philistine. Denial of the play's political implications (in itself a political stance) also sentimentalized the peasantry into art and thus took the side of the artist against the middle-class audience. It gave power to the artist to represent peasant life, to turn characters into linguistic elements, and to control Irish mythology. The placement of Irish life in the artist's domain has been possible largely because later audiences have manifested different politics and because the political feature of dramatizing the peasantry has changed or dropped out altogether as the historical situation has changed. This situation has in turn made it possible for critics to interpret the ironic and aggressive nature of the play as part of its playfulness and artistic extravagance. It is in this sense that critics have not only accepted the Yeatsian premises about *The Playboy,* but also defended the play against the original audience without understanding how the text was written in opposition to that audience. The result, however, both defends and domesticates the play. Rereading *The Playboy* in terms of its historical context therefore restores to the text its original power and audacity.

It is necessary to remember that the relationship between the playwright and his audience is mediated by the actors who develop their own interpretive strategies for embodying and presenting a text. With regard to *The Playboy,* this intervention has usually meant emphasizing either the naturalistic mode or the mode of grotesque extravagance. By choosing to privilege one mode at the expense of the other, the actors re-create the play in that image. William Fay, who played the original Christy Mahon, made clear his own interpretation of the play when he stated that Synge "was apt to think in terms of Zola, who got his effects by keeping all his characters in one key." Padraic Colum believed that Fay made the role too "sardonic" and that this bias undermined "the extravagance of the comedy," thus contributing to the trouble with the audience. Synge himself called Fay's performance "pretty bluffy." Although Synge helped Fay and the other Abbey actors during rehearsals, it may be—as Ann Saddlemyer has suggested—that they misread his somewhat obscure wishes as a demand for more realism. As a result, he partially blamed them for glossing the play's "subtleties."

Since then, the Irish actor Cyril Cusack, who acted the part of

Christy on and off from 1936–55, has argued that *The Playboy* demands an acting style compounding "the purely theatrical with a form of naturalism perilously near to being simply representational, two apparently conflicting elements which nonetheless are present and compatible in the work of Synge." But the two radically different responses to *The Playboy* suggest that these two elements are not necessarily compatible. The conflict between pure theatricality and naturalism is something like the contradictory portraits of Pegeen Mike suggested by Christy and the Widow Quin. Whereas Christy, in a famous image culled from Gaelic love poetry, sees "the love-light of the star of knowledge shining from her brow," the Widow Quin can find only "a girl you'd see itching and scratching, and she with a stale stink of poteen on her from selling in the shop." These two contradictory (and equally accurate) portraits of Pegeen exist simultaneously, and *The Playboy* valorizes both of them. Which Pegeen one sees depends on who is doing the looking and who is acting.

In his celebrated preface, Synge suggests that "On the stage one must have reality, and one must have joy," and since the original production critics have periodically pointed out the difficult relationship between prose naturalism ("reality") and poetic extravagance ("joy") in the play. Without resolving these antinomies, both the dialogue and the plot continually pose the language of empiricism against the language of aspiration. It has generally been ignored that these two different modes have given rise and textual license to two opposing strategies for interpreting *The Playboy*. One is tempted to call them the historical and the aesthetic, though every historical response is tied to an aesthetic one and every aesthetic response has historical implications. The conflict between these two traditions is mirrored in the text itself and in the relationship between two radically different modes of discourse: the comic language of farce continually challenges the play's empirical conventions, and vice versa. The play is problematic precisely because it insistently creates a way of responding to it which it then contradicts. To foreground the drama's linguistic and aesthetic plenitude is to deny its representational implications; to try to fit the grotesque or theatrical discourse into a representational framework is to deny the play's aesthetic code. These strategies lead to different evaluations of the play as either a comic masterpiece or a failed representation. And these antitheses may be another way of saying that *The Playboy* is both "a gallous story" and "a dirty deed."

The Living World for Text:
The Playboy

Hugh Kenner

When John Quinn, in New York, thought of buying the *Playboy* manuscript Synge described what it was like.

> I work always with a typewriter—typing myself—so I suppose it has no value? I make a rough draft first and then work over it with a pen until it is nearly unreadable; then I make a clean draft again, adding whatever seems wanting, and so on. My final drafts—I letter them as I go along— were "G" for the first act, "I" for the second, and "K" for the third! I really wrote parts of the last act more than eleven times, as I often took out individual scenes and worked at them separately. The MS., as it now stands, is a good deal written over, and some of it is in slips or strips only, cut from the earlier versions—so I do not know whether it has any interest for the collector.

It had; and the typescript Quinn bought is now at Indiana University. Later Synge made two more drafts of act 2, so the Indiana copy is "K."

The plays gained density slowly. A notebook draft of what was still called "The Fool of Farnham" has the pubkeeper's daughter writing out an order: "Three barrels of porter with the best compliments of the season." (Synge disliked using any but authentic phrases, and "wishing you the best compliments of this season" was a flourish from a letter a girl on Aran wrote him.) By typescript "D"

From *A Colder Eye: The Modern Irish Writers.* © 1983 by Hugh Kenner. Alfred A. Knopf, 1983.

117

this had become "Two dozens of Powers Whiskey. Three barrels of porter. And soda as before." In the margin of draft "E" (May 23, 1905) he prompted himself: "Open out? Try making her order her trouseau?" and flipping the page he jotted a trousseau: "Six yards of yellow silk ribbon, a pair of long boots, bright hat suited for a young woman on her wedding day, a fine tooth comb to be sent." His pen hovered over this. "Long boots" became "pair of shoes with English heels"; then "English" became "big," "big" became "long," "long" became "lengthy," and in the printed text that copies typescript "G" *The Playboy of the Western World* begins:

> PEGEEN (*slowly, as she writes*): Six yards of stuff for to make a yellow gown. A pair of lace boots with lengthy heels on them and brassy eyes. A hat is suited for a wedding day. A fine tooth comb. To be sent with two barrels of porter in Jimmy Farrell's creel cart on the evening of the coming Fair to Mister Michael James Flaherty. With the best compliments of this season: Margaret Flaherty.

Sharp eyes will notice that "the season" became "this season," exactly the wording of the letter of the girl from Aran. No detail was too minute for pondering. As late as the final typescript of act 3 the "drift of chosen females" was standing "stripped itself," and when Synge at the last minute draped them in the notorious shifts he thought he had adjusted an outrageousness. His model was the thirty virgins arrayed in the old story, to quench Cuchulain's bloody rage with the sight of their stark nakedness: the hero paid them nearly Victorian courtesy.

Some elements were never changed at all. One of the things he knew from the first about his playboy hero was that his name was Christy: a mock-Christ who puts an end to crucifixion by killing the Father. Brought up in a scriptural family which had even preceded him to the Aran Islands in the person of a reverend uncle with a mission to reform papists' ways ("I have succeeded in putting a stop to the ball match that used to go on here every Sunday"—1851), the sardonic John Millington Synge made free in his plays with scriptural motifs. *The Well of the Saints* is about a canonical miracle, blindness cured, which proves unwanted ("It's a power of dirty days, and dark mornings, and shabby-looking fellows we do have to be looking on when we have our sight"). *In the Shadow of the Glen* turns on a resurrection, also unwanted; when the "dead" husband leaps from his bed no one present, including his wife, is anything but chagrined. And *The Playboy* has a resurrection too, for good measure a pair of them, the slain and risen figure both times not the son but the father, whom Synge after several deleted tries surnamed Mahon, pronounced Ma'on, approximately Man: not a "meaning," no, an agnostic author at play.

In this topsy-turvy gospel Christy the Son of Mahon was as abstemious as you'd want ("poor fellow would get drunk on the smell of a pint") and so chaste he ran from the sight of a distant girl (when "you'd see him shooting out his sheep's eyes between the little twigs and the leaves") and indeed had every virtue you can list save being any use; and when his old rascal of a father instructed him that his next move in life, after these potatoes were dug, should be to wed the Widow Casey, Christy would have none of that idea at all. For the Widow Casey was "a walking terror from beyond the hills, and she two score and five years, and two hundredweights on her, and a blinded eye, and she a woman of noted misbehaviour with the old and young." In all but not being skinny she was the Sheela-na-gig, the old Irish effort at a fertility goddess, a skeleton with huge pudenda, grinning like death.

So Christy banged his father with the spade, saying later he'd split his skull to the knob of his gullet and still later that he'd split him to the breeches belt; but in fact by the word of the resurrected father, "Weren't you off racing the hills before I got my breath with the start I had seeing you turn on me at all?"

That was in Kerry, where the Kerrymen come from about whom the Irish tell their Polish jokes; the way the Kerryman broke his leg was he fell out of the tree raking leaves, so you know murder is a thing he'd botch. Christy next ran and walked for eleven days all the way north to the mean bleak country toward Belmullet in County Mayo. (Did it amuse Synge, as it would have amused James Joyce, that to get there he must have trudged past Lady Gregory's Coole?)

Northwest Mayo was a sinister overpopulated wilderness, bogs, stones and hovels, the heart of the Congested Districts that stretched down the Atlantic coast from Donegal to Dingle and were the special concern of a Board charged with bureaucratic countermeasures to starvation. This blind corner of Ireland stunned even the optimistic Æ. It was from Belmullet itself Æ had written to Synge in 1897 how he was disheartened out of words. There was nothing to write about save the distress and that was "a disgrace to humanity" and "not cheerful subject matter for a letter."

Synge was first in Belmullet in September 1904, and made there the first sketches for all three acts of "The Murderer (A Farce)," four titles later *The Playboy of the Western World*. The people thereabouts, his journal recalls, were "debased and nearly demoralized by bad housing and lodging and the endless misery and rain." Any girl's usual costume was "a short red petticoat over bare feet and legs, a faded uncertain bodice and a white or blue rag swathing the head," and the town was "squalid and noisy, lonely and crowded at the same time and without any appeal to the imagination." It was in a like place he heard an old boatman's lament: "I don't know what way I'm going to go on living in this place that the Lord created last, I'm thinking, in the end of time; and it's often when I sit down and look around on it I do begin cursing and damning, and asking myself how poor people can go on executing their religion at all." That was the Western World, so called to contrast it with the Dublin or eastern side of the island, and Christy Mahon fetches up there. Nowhere was it less likely that the pure and exalted peasantry of Nationalist myth might be found, chaste in action, chaste in speech, united in simple love of Ireland and Holy Church and Father Reilly.

That was true even if Synge had been content to depict them naturalistically. The region had a long history of strife. It was there in 1880 that Captain Boycott got boycotted, and that was a mild dealing. Reprisals were normally brutal. Twenty-nine Mayo men, by a story Synge heard there and made a ballad of, once decided it was high time to deal with a hell-raiser named Danny, 'd capsize the stars:

> "But we'll come round him in the night
> A mile beyond the Mullet;
> Ten will quench his bloody eyes,
> And ten will choke his gullet."

W. B. Yeats's sister Lollie declined to set this in type. Synge's ballad particularized what damage Danny did the lads who ambushed him, but it was dozens to one, and

> seven tripped him up behind
> And seven kicked before,
> And seven squeezed around his throat
> Till Danny kicked no more.

Then some destroyed him with their heels,
Some tramped him in the mud,
Some stole his purse and timber-pipe,
And some washed off his blood.

. . . .

And when you're walking out the way
From Bangor to Belmullet,
You'll see a flat cross on a stone
Where men choked Danny's gullet.

The pious X-marks-the-spot is a fine touch. And between Belmullet and Bangor, that would not be far off from where we might look for the *shebeen* (low pub) Christy Mahon, reputed murderer, stumbles into after getting his wind in a ditch.

Synge's first thought had been to dramatize a story he was told on Aran, about how folk in a remote place will shelter a fugitive. When W. B. Yeats himself first visited Aran in 1896 there were islanders who thought from his oblique eye he was a killer in need of refuge instead of a tourist with a skew cornea. "If any gentleman has done a crime we'll hide him," Yeats was told meaningfully. And an old man, the oldest on Inishmaan, more than once told Synge a story out of living memory "about a Connaught man who killed his father with the blow of a spade when he was in a passion, and then fled to this island and threw himself on the mercy of some of the natives. . . . They hid him in a hole—which the old man shown me—and kept him safe for a week, though the police came and searched for him, and he could hear their boots grinding on the stones over his head." Then they got him off to America. Synge reflected:

> This impulse to protect the criminal is universal in the west. . . . Such a man, they say, will be quiet all the rest of his life, and if you suggest that punishment is needed as an example, they ask, "Would any one kill his father if he was able to help it?"

But the first sketches he set down in Belmullet in late 1904 already eschew this sententious note. He had commenced to amuse himself with the notion of a folk who might not simply shield a murderer but glorify him. For whom did Irishmen glorify? Looking round at their current heroes he saw Fenians, the Phoenix Park mur-

derers—thugs, dynamiters, knifers; also the literary cult of Cuchulain the skull-basher.

So in act 1 we should see the bang on the head itself, out in that
Kerry potato field. Then in act 2—this was pivotal—the murderer
would be a feisty talker; himself it was would dictate the terms of
glory. He would tell of the deed at every provocation, and his eloquence would boss the show. They would elect him county
councillor! (When Synge was feeling sardonic his thoughts turned
ritually to politicians, though never did any of these windbags sur-
vive into a finished play.) In act 3 the father—not dead after all—
would turn up to spoil the victory speech by calling his son a liar.
"Son attacks father and is handcuffed." This was "The Murderer (A
Farce)," and whether Synge judged it more farcical to disgrace this
politician or reinstate him we cannot know, since the next leaf is torn
from the notebook.

It is trivial, but so are all Synge's projects in the notebook stage
beyond which most of them were never carried. His way, in four of
the six plays he finished—the exceptions are *Deirdre* and *Riders to the
Sea*—was to start from something like a sophomore's joke and
endow it slowly with human range and weight: blind folk who trea-
sure their blindness, dead men who will not stay dead, tinkers who
crave the blessing of the parish priest and end up tying him in a sack.
It was while *The Playboy* was still a *jeu d'esprit* that he let a simple
point of stagecraft impose a crucial decision. The opening scene, the
killing in the potato field, was deleted. For to keep an audience from
seeing the blank side walls of the Abbey's box a set-dresser would
have to arrange canvas frames, called wings, on which he would have
painted—what but trees? So, as Yeats explained to an audience at
Harvard, "Synge gave up the intention of showing upon the stage a
fight between 'The Playboy' and his father, because he would not
have six large trees, three on each side, growing in the middle of a
ploughed field." That was impeccable Irish logic.

Consequently *The Playboy* has but the one set, the shebeen
Pegeen helps her father run, and now Synge was able to get inter-
ested in an idea he might otherwise have dropped, since we in the
audience no longer know what happened in the field as we listen to
Christy, so his eloquence can work on us the way it does on the men
and girls of Mayo. This greatly alters the effect envisaged in "The
Murderer," where we'd have seen a braggart inflaming silly folk
we were free to feel superior to. Now Christy's talk can create an
heroic world.

CHRISTY (*impressively*): With that the sun came out between the cloud and the hill, and it shining green in
my face. "God have mercy on your soul," says he,
lifting a scythe. "Or on your own," says I, raising
the loy.

SUSAN: That's a grand story.

HONOR: He tells it lovely.

CHRISTY (*flattered and confident, waving bone*): He gave a
drive with the scythe, and I gave a lep to the east.
Then I turned around with my back to the north,
and I hit a blow on the ridge of his skull, laid him
stretched out, and he split to the knob of his gullet.
(*He raises the chicken bone to his Adam's apple*).

GIRLS (*together*): Well, you're a marvel! Oh, God bless
you! You're the lad surely!

Indeed it's a grand story and he tells it lovely, guided by a playwright
who knew with what ceremonies of formal speech and specificity of
clinical detail *The Iliad* tells such things, or how Ulysses, famous for
his lies, entranced the Phaiacians over drinks with wondrous tales.
The equipoise between language and heroics in Homer would eventually occupy Joyce, and Synge had no doubt that eloquence the like
of Nora Burke's tramp's could limn for the deprived some land of
heart's desire. *The Playboy,* one of the first self-cancelling plays, is a
great iridescent bubble we watch blown, and admire till the moment
it bursts, and regret after. It is we, and not only Pegeen in that forlorn
last speech, who have lost the only Playboy of the Western World.
We shall have him back as surely as the curtain can be persuaded to
rise on another performance.

But tucks will appear in a fabric however well woven. If on the
opening night the wrongness that offended the patriots was not
wrong with the play but with their ideology, still there was something else wrong, to be sensed as dogs sense ozone far from thunder,
and that was a subtle wrongness with Synge's whole sense of even the
most brutalized Catholic peasantry. Though he used, he said, barely
a word that he hadn't heard, still it was by him the words were
arranged, and the oaths and invocations seem not so much overnu-
merous as disconcertingly placed. They bubble at the crests of
good-humored vigor; and a cheerful vigor in that continuum of poverty is the daydream of a scion of Bible-readers who trusts that
elsewhere, despite all, there exist people the rhythm of whose "Prov-

idence and Mercy, spare us all!" bespeaks chthonic energies.

Among such people there will be poltroons of course, afeard of Father Reilly and fussing about a dispensation to marry; that was a way to characterize Shawn Keogh, and it did not trouble Synge that there was no intelligible reason why a dispensation should be needed. Professor Henn thinks it is necessary because Pegeen and Shawn are being married in Lent, but Lent is in March and Synge's note beneath the list of characters states plainly that the play is set in the autumn. No, "dispensation" for Synge is a piece of Papist rigmarole Father Reilly can worry Shawn Keogh with: a trivial detail but indicative of a surface beneath which his knowledge of Kerry and Mayo did not penetrate.

Or cast a cold eye on the speech with which Pegeen's father greets Christy in act 3:

> The blessing of God and the holy angels on your head, young fellow. I hear tell you're after winning all in the sports below; and wasn't it a shame I didn't bear you along with me to Kate Cassidy's wake, a fine stout lad, the like of you, for you'd never see the match of it for flows of drink, the way when we sunk her bones at noonday in her narrow grave, there were five men, aye, and six men, strained out retching speechless on the holy stones.

That is not the talk of the Congested Districts but of a fantasy land as like Mayo as Shakespeare's bear-plagued seacoast of Bohemia is like the Adriatic strand. Shakespeare had the advantage over Synge, that no one from Bohemia was likely to be at the Globe.

The speech assembles much verifiable detail: that spirits flow at a wake, that one measure of a spirituous deluge is the body-count of the prostrate, that these if conscious will retch, that a grave is narrow, that God and the holy angels may get ceremonially invoked. Yet as the utterance of a Mayo pubkeeper it is implausible, and Synge though he defended his local accuracies ("one or two words only that I have not heard") never claimed a play made of such speeches was plausible. "An extravaganza," he said, and we'd best believe him, noting how like are its mechanics to those of well-made French farce, abundant in contrivances to hustle someone—in France the deceived husband, here the aggrieved father—back and forth through doors so he'll not meet someone else.

Synge's extravagances are propelled by his love of dizzying contrasts:

MAHON (*With hesitation*): What's that? they're raising him
    up. They're coming this way. (*With a roar of rage
    and astonishment*) It's Christy, by the stars of God!
    I'd know his way of spitting and he astride the moon.

This has literary analogues more cogent than the dubious folk ones
Synge half-claimed. The stars of God, spitting, the moon: heteroge-
neous ideas yoked by violence together: a taste for such effects was
coalescing, and we may reflect that the play was finished only six
years before Grierson's edition of Donne inaugurated the new century's resurrection of that yeasty poet. "Metaphysical" qualities have
since been noted in the way Jimmy Farrell tells how madness is a
fright:

It's a fright, surely. I knew a party was kicked in the head
by a red mare, and he went killing horses a great while, till
he eat the insides of a clock and died after.

Horses, an indigestible clock: if we think of lovers and a pair of "stiff
twin compasses" we spot something astir in the sensibility of that
decade, that would soon welcome "A Valediction, Forbidding
Mourning," despised nearly two hundred years. Or "The Re-
lique":

When my grave is broke up again
Some second guest to entertain
—For graves have learned that woman-head
To be to more than one a bed—
    And he that digs it, spies
A bracelet of bright hair about the bone.

Soon T. S. Eliot would marvel at the "telescoping of images," "the
sudden contrast of associations of 'bright hair' and of 'bone,' " and in
a similar connection would adduce "that surprise which has been one
of the most important means of poetic effect since Homer," poetic
effect having been delivered from Tennyson. Yeats concurred.
"Donne could be as metaphysical as he pleased . . . because he could
be as physical as he pleased." And Synge:

—Did you ever hear tell of the skulls they have in the
city of Dublin, ranged out like blue jars in a cabin of Connaught?
—And you believe that?

—Didn't a lad see them, and he after coming from har-
vesting in the Liverpool boat? "They have them there,"
says he, "making a show of the great people there was one
time walking the world. White skulls and black skulls and
yellow skulls, and some with full teeth, and some haven't
only but one."

—It's no lie, maybe, for when I was a young lad there
was a graveyard beyond the house with the remnants of a
man who had thighs as long as your arm. He was a horrid
man, I'm telling you, and there was many a fine Sunday I'd
put him together for fun, and he with shiny bones, you
wouldn't meet the like of these days in the cities of the
world.

He labored through many drafts of a poem for his fiancée Molly
Allgood that evokes near a churchyard full of whitening bones a
sexual resurrection of the body. In verse, though, he was too near the
Victorians to attempt direct speech save at the bony lines. In one draft
we find,

> With what new gold you'd gilded all the moon
> With what rare anthem raised the river's tune
> Where bees fetch honey for their swarming cribs
> And we're two skulls and backs and forty ribs.

Meter, until the skulls and ribs poke through, confines him in Geor-
gian diction; he was right to give up his early fumblings toward verse
drama. It was out of rhythms the pentameter does not permit that his
idiosyncratic effects arose.

Yet a governing rhythm, which entails a convention for speaking, was one ground of Elizabethan stage success, and Synge's high
ambitions left him soon uncontented with anything less than a modern equivalent. Yeats noted as early as *The Well of the Saints* that "all
his people would change their life if the rhythm changed," and *The
Playboy,* so often rewritten in quest of a form for its verbal designs,
offers one audacious experiment, the presence from the opening
words to the closing of a persistent recurrent tune, an Irish tune with
remote Gaelic credentials, marked by a rhythmic figure that troubles
actors because its jaunty beat can be neither obeyed nor suppressed.
When Yeats wrote that Synge "made word and phrase dance to a
very strange rhythm," difficult for players "till his plays have created
their own tradition," *The Playboy* was still in the making, and no

actor had yet confronted the challenge of delivering Christy Mahon's exit-speech, that summation of a romping future with his da:

> CHRISTY: Ten thousand blessings upon all that's here, for
> you've turned me a likely gaffer in the end of all,
> the way I'll go romancing through a romping life-
> time from this hour to the dawning of the Judge-
> ment Day.

Something wants to force the last clauses into a quatrain:

> The way I'll go romancing
> through a romping lifetime
> from this hour to the dawning
> of the <u>Judge</u> <u>ment</u> <u>Day</u>.

Nor is that unique; more are easily collected.

> I did not then.
> Oh, they're bloody liars
> in the naked parish
> where I grew a man.

Each of the following is within a page of the next:

> It should have been great
> and bitter torment
> did rouse your spirits
> to a <u>deed</u> <u>of</u> <u>blood</u>.

> That was a sneaky
> kind of murder
> did win small glory
> with the <u>boys</u> <u>it</u> <u>self</u>.

> And that there isn't
> my match in Mayo
> for thatching, or mowing,
> or shearing a sheep.

> Till I'm thinking this night
> wasn't I a foolish fellow
> not to kill my father
> in the <u>years</u> <u>gone</u> <u>by</u>.

These are all from act 1, and once we have picked up the pattern—

three syncopated measures, then a thudding three-stress termination—we may come to think it omnipresent. We may even find its elements, with free interpolation dividing them, in Pegeen's opening words:

> Six yards of stuff
> for to make a yellow gown
> A pair of lace boots with lengthy
> heels on them and brassy eyes.
> A hat is suited
> for a <u>wed</u> <u>ding</u> <u>day</u>.

"For a <u>wed</u> | <u>ding</u> | <u>day</u>"; "in the y<u>ears</u> | <u>gone</u> | <u>by</u>"; "of the <u>Judge</u> | <u>ment</u> | <u>Day</u>"; that triple terminal beat: where can we have heard it before? It is possible we are remembering its debasement in the anthology piece about the bells of Shandon on the <u>ri</u> | <u>ver</u> | <u>Lee</u>.

> On this I ponder
> Where'er I wander
> And thus grow fonder,
>   Sweet Cork, of thee:
> With thy bells of Shandon
> That sound so grand on
>   The pleasant waters
>   Of the river Lee.

Those over-familiar lines of Francis Mahony (1804–66) dance to a persistent tune indeed: they echo "The Groves of Blarney" by Richard Milliken (1767–1815), who was parodying something anonymous called "Castlehyde," which went to Irish music that once had Gaelic words, now lost. Synge was a fiddler. Did he somewhere pick up the old tune? Was it merely "The Bells of Shandon" that rang in his head?

Surely not. Fiddle-music or no, he could have found Irish assonantal stanzas like the one that degenerated into "Shandon" exhibited in Douglas Hyde's *Songs Ascribed to Raftery* (1903), with deft English imitations, as for instance:

> There's a lovely posy lives by the roadway
>   Deirdre was nowhere beside my joy,
> Nor Helen who boasted of conquests Trojan,
>   For whom was roasted the town of Troy.

Try that again: "The <u>town</u> | <u>of</u> | <u>Troy</u>": "for a <u>wed</u> | <u>ding</u> | <u>day</u>": yes, it's close. A folk rhythm, then, known to Sassenachs in its "Bells of Shandon" debasement.

That he built this rhythm (and others) into speech after speech of *The Playboy* is indisputable. How he judged it we cannot know. Like much other Irish, it had been rendered banal already by English parody. A banality, then, to establish Christy's banality? A lilt, to endear? More likely, a token of how Christy and his da and Pegeen and the rest are bound into one community of lilting rogues.

Had he lived we'd know more of the drama he intuited: prose knitted by cross-rhythms insistent as any verse. He wrote but six plays, and in a brief time, 1902–9, the last months of which were also taken up with dying. William Shakespeare's sixth play (of thirty-odd) was merely *Titus Andronicus*.

Chronology

1871   Edmund John Millington Synge born on April 10 in Rathfarnham, near Dublin, Ireland. His father, a barrister, dies the following year.

1881   Attends a private school for four years, then studies under a tutor at home. A few years later, after reading Darwin, Synge moves away from his mother's evangelical Christianity and becomes agnostic.

1888–92   Enrolls in the Royal Irish Academy of Music and Trinity College, Dublin. During these years, Parnell dies, and the Irish Literary Society is founded by Yeats in London and Dublin. Synge graduates with a pass B.A. from Trinity, where he studied languages, and with music scholarships from the Academy.

1893–98   Visits Germany to study music, but soon moves to Paris, where he studies Gaelic, French, and Italian at the Sorbonne. Meets Yeats in Paris in 1896 and is associated with *L'Association Irlandaise* for a short time. Synge is operated on for Hodgkins disease. He develops a friendship with Stephen McKenna, and in 1898 makes his first visit to the Aran Islands.

1898–1902   Spends much of his time in Paris and every summer on the Aran Islands. Joins Yeats and Lady Gregory in developing the Irish National Theatre Society.

1903   First production of *In the Shadow of the Glen*.

1904   First performance of *Riders to the Sea*. The Abbey Theatre is founded.

1905   First production of *The Well of the Saints*. Synge becomes a member of the Abbey Theatre Board of Directors.

1906   Engaged to actress Molly Allgood (Maire O'Neill).

1907   First production of *The Playboy of the Western World*
        causes riots at the Abbey Theatre. Publication of *The
        Aran Islands*.

1908   Death of Synge's mother. Synge is operated on for a
        tumor.

1909   Dies in Dublin on March 24. First production of *The
        Tinker's Wedding* in Dublin; publication of *Poems and
        Translations*.

1910   First production of *Deirdre of the Sorrows* (left uncom-
        pleted at Synge's death) at the Abbey Theatre; publi-
        cation of the first edition of Synge's *Collected Works*.

Contributors

HAROLD BLOOM, Sterling Professor of the Humanities at Yale University, is the author of *The Anxiety of Influence, Poetry and Repression,* and many other volumes of literary criticism. His forthcoming study, *Freud: Transference and Authority,* attempts a full-scale reading of all of Freud's major writings. A MacArthur Prize Fellow, he is general editor of five series of literary criticism published by Chelsea House. During 1987–88, he served as Charles Eliot Norton Professor of Poetry at Harvard University.

PATRICIA MEYER SPACKS is Professor of English and Chairman of the English Department at Yale University. She is the author of many essays and books; among the latter are *Imagining a Self: Autobiography and Novel in Eighteenth-Century England, The Female Imagination,* and *Gossip.*

ALAN PRICE is Senior Lecturer in Education at Queen's University, Belfast. He has written extensively on Irish literature, and his books include *Synge and Anglo-Irish Drama* and *Riders to the Sea, The Playboy of the Western World,* as well as an edition of Synge's prose.

DONNA GERSTENBERGER is Professor of English at the University of Washington. She has co-authored several volumes of the *Directory of Periodicals* and *The American Novel: A Checklist of Twentieth-Century Criticism,* and has written on Synge, Iris Murdoch, and women writers.

ROBIN SKELTON is Professor of English at the University of Victoria, B.C., and has written several books, including *J. M. Synge, The Poet's Calling,* and *Poetic Truth.*

NICHOLAS GRENE is Fellow and Director of Studies in Modern English at Trinity College, Dublin. In addition to a critical study of

Shaw, he has written *Shakespeare, Jonson, Molière: The Comic Contract* and *Synge: A Critical Study of the Plays*.

BRUCE M. BIGLEY is Assistant Professor of English at the University of Montana. He has written on the transformations in European drama from 1880 to 1920, focusing on Ibsen, Synge, and von Hofmannsthal.

EDWARD HIRSCH teaches in the English Department at Wayne State University. His book of poems, *For the Sleepwalkers,* appeared as part of the Knopf Poetry Series in 1981, and he has written a number of essays on Irish literature and folklore.

HUGH KENNER, Professor of English at The Johns Hopkins University, is the recipient of several awards, including the Porter Prize and the Christian Gauss Prize. His books include *Samuel Beckett, Dublin's Joyce,* and *The Invisible Poet: T. S. Eliot.*

Bibliography

Agostini, René. "A Reading of John Millington Synge's *The Playboy of the Western World:* The Problem of Identity." *Cahiers Victoriens et Edouardiens* 9–10 (1979): 253–71.

Akin, Warren. " 'I Just Riz the Loy': The Oedipal Dimension of *The Playboy of the Western World*." *South Atlantic Bulletin* 45, no. 4 (1980): 55–65.

Bessai, Diane E. "The Little Hound of Mayo: Synge's *Playboy* and the Comic Tradition of Irish Literature." *The Drama Review* 48 (1968): 372–83.

Bowen, Zack. "Padraic Colum and Irish Drama." *Eire-Ireland: A Journal of Irish Studies* 5, no. 4 (1970): 71–82.

Bushrui, S. B., ed. *Sunshine and the Moon's Delight: A Centenary Tribute to John Millington Synge.* Gerrards Cross, Ireland: Colin Smythe, 1972.

Canfield, Fayette Curtis, ed. *Plays of the Irish Renaissance, 1880–1930.* New York: Washburn, 1929.

Edwards, Bernard L. "The Vision of J. M. Synge: A study of *The Playboy of the Western World.*" *English Literature in Transition (1880–1920)* 17 (1974): 8–18.

Ganz, Arthur. "J. M. Synge and the Drama of Art." *Modern Drama* 10 (May 1967): 57–68.

———. "John M. Synge: The Refuge of Art." In *Realms of the Self: Variations on a Theme in Modern Drama.* New York: New York University Press, 1980.

Gerstenberger, Donna. *John Millington Synge.* New York: Twayne, 1964.

Grene, Nicholas. *Synge: A Critical Study of the Plays.* London: Macmillan, 1975.

Hart, William. "Synge's Ideas on Life and Art: Design and Theory in *The Playboy of the Western World.*" *Yeats Studies* 2 (1972): 33–51.

Hogan, Robert. *After the Irish Renaissance: A Critical History of Irish Drama since* The Plough and the Stars. Minneapolis: University of Minnesota Press, 1967.

———. "An Interview with Michael Conniffe." *The Journal of Irish Literature* 6, no. 3 (1977): 80–88.

Johnson, Toni O'Brien. *Synge: The Medieval and the Grotesque.* Totowa, N.J.: Barnes & Noble, 1982.

Kenner, Hugh. *A Colder Eye: The Modern Irish Writers.* New York: Knopf, 1983.

Kiberd, Declan. "The Fall of the Stage Irishman." *Genre* 12 (Winter 1979): 458–61.

———. *Synge and the Irish Language.* London: Macmillan, 1979.

Kilroy, James. "The Playboy as Poet." *PMLA* 83 (May 1968): 439–42.

———. *The Playboy Riots*. Dublin: Dolmen, 1971.

King, Mary C. *The Drama of J. M. Synge*. London: Fourth Estate, 1985.

Levitt, Paul M. "The Two-Act Structure of *The Playboy of the Western World*." *Colby Library Quarterly* 11 (1975): 230–34.

Nethercot, Arthur H. *"The Playboy of the Western World."* *Eire-Ireland: A Journal of Irish Studies* 13, no. 2 (1978): 114–20.

Parker, Randolph R. "Gaming in the Gap: Language and Liminality in *Playboy of the Western World*." *Theatre Journal* 37, no. 1 (March 1985): 65–85.

Pearce, Howard D. "Synge's Playboy as Mock Christ." *Modern Drama* 8 (1965): 303–10.

Pierce, James C. "Synge's Widow Quin: Touchstone to the *Playboy*'s Irony." *Eire-Ireland: A Journal of Irish Studies,* 16, no. 2 (1981): 122–33.

Price, Alan. *Synge and Anglo-Irish Drama*. New York: Russell & Russell, 1972.

Rollins, Ronald G. "Huckleberry Finn and Christy Mahon: *The Playboy of the Western World*." *Mark Twain Journal* 13, no. 2 (1966): 16–19.

Saddlemeyer, Ann. *J. M. Synge and Modern Comedy*. Dublin: Dolmen, 1968.

———. "Synge and the Doors of Perception." In *Place, Personality and the Irish Writer,* edited by Andrew Carpenter, 97–120. Gerrards Cross, Ireland: Colin Smythe, 1977.

Sahal, N. *Sixty Years of Realistic Irish Drama*. Bombay: Macmillan, 1971.

Sidnell, M. J. "Synge's *Playboy* and the Champion of Ulster." *Dalhousie Review* 45 (Spring 1965): 51–59.

Skelton, Robin. *The Writings of J. M. Synge*. New York: Bobbs-Merrill, 1971.

Skelton, Robin, and Ann Saddlemeyer, eds. *The World of W. B. Yeats*. Seattle: University of Washington Press, 1965.

Sullivan, Mary Rose. "Synge, Sophocles, and the Unmaking of Myth." *Modern Drama* 12 (December 1969): 242–53.

Watson, Ernest Bradlee, comp. *Contemporary Drama*. New York: Scribner's, 1966.

Whitaker, Thomas R., ed. *Twentieth Century Interpretations of* The Playboy of the Western World: *A Collection of Critical Essays*. Englewood Cliffs, N.J.: Prentice-Hall, 1969.

Acknowledgments

"The Making of the Playboy" by Patricia Meyer Spacks from *Modern Drama* 4, no. 3 (December 1961), © 1961 by the University of Toronto, Graduate Centre for the Study of Drama. Reprinted by permission of *Modern Drama*.

"The Dramatic Imagination: *The Playboy*" (originally entitled "Longer Plays: *The Playboy of the Western World*") by Alan Price from *Synge and Anglo-Irish Drama* by Alan Price, © 1961 by Alan Price. Reprinted with the permission of Russell & Russell, a division of Atheneum Publishers, an imprint of Macmillan Publishing Company.

"A Hard Birth" by Donna Gerstenberger from *John Millington Synge* by Donna Gerstenberger, © 1964 by Twayne Publishers, Inc. Reprinted by permission of Twayne Publishers, a division of G. K. Hall & Co., Boston.

"Character and Symbol" (originally entitled *"The Playboy of the Western World"*) by Robin Skelton from *The Writings of J. M. Synge* by Robin Skelton, © 1971 by The Bobbs-Merrill Company, Inc. Reprinted by permission.

"Approaches to *The Playboy*" by Nicholas Grene from *Synge: A Critical Study of the Plays* by Nicholas Grene, © 1975 Nicholas Grene. Reprinted by permission of Macmillan Press Ltd.

"The Playboy as Antidrama" (originally entitled *"The Playboy of the Western World* as Antidrama") by Bruce M. Bigley from *Modern Drama* 20, no. 2 (June 1977), © 1977 by the University of Toronto, Graduate Centre for the Study of Drama. Reprinted by permission of *Modern Drama*.

"The Gallous Story and the Dirty Deed: The Two *Playboys*" by Edward Hirsch from *Modern Drama* 26, no. 1 (March 1983), © 1983 by the University of Toronto, Graduate Centre for the Study of Drama. Reprinted by permission of *Modern Drama*.

"The Living World for Text: *The Playboy*" by Hugh Kenner from *A Colder Eye: The Modern Irish Writers* by Hugh Kenner, © 1983 by Hugh Kenner. Reprinted by permission of Penguin Books Ltd. and Alfred A. Knopf, Inc.

Index